CONTENTS

OLYMPICS '96

Written by
Neil Morris

PUFFIN BOOKS

Acknowledgments
Illustrators Clive Spong
Gerald Whitcomb (Specs Art)
Designed by Sally Boothroyd

The Complete-Your-Own Results Tables and how they work

the event

name and country of the Olympic-record holder

name and country of the 1992 gold-medal winner

on some tables the 1992 gold-medal winners are listed under one heading

name and country of an individual winner

| ○ 110 m HURDLES | 1992 WINNER M.McKoy (Can) |
| OLYMPIC RECORD R.Kingdom (USA) 12.98 | |

(1)   Time:
(2)   Time:
(3)   Time:

| ○ 400 m HURDLES | 1992 WINNER K.Young (USA) |
| OLYMPIC RECORD K.Young (USA) 46.78 | |

(1)   Time:
(2)   Time:
(3)   Time:

WOMEN	1992 WINNERS
○ K-1 500 m	B.Schmidt (GER)
(1)	Time:
○ K-2 500 m	R.Portwich & A.Von Seck (GER)
(1)	Time:
○ K-4 500 m	HUN
(1)	Time:
○ K-1 slalom	E.Micheler (GER)
(1)	Time:

(1) denotes gold, (2) denotes silver and (3) denotes bronze

space to fill in the names of the gold-medal winner, the silver-medal winner and the bronze-medal winner

space to fill in the name of the gold-medal winner

space to fill in the winning time

a team winner is shown by its country

• rapid fire pistol 25 m • small bore rifle prone
50 m • small bore rifle, 3 positions 50 m • running
game target 10 m • air rifle 10 m • air pistol
10 m • trap • double trap • skeet
women's events: • pistol match 25 m • air rifle
10 m • air pistol 10 m • small bore rifle,
3 positions 50 m • double trap
archery men's events: • individual round
(90-70-50-30 m) • team event
women's events: • individual round (70-60-50-30 m)
• team event

ATLANTA, GEORGIA
**Home of the Centennial Olympic Games
July 19 – August 4, 1996**

The XXVI Olympiad is being held in Atlanta, the
state capital and largest city of Georgia, in the
south-east of the United States. Atlanta was
founded in 1837 as a small rail town, growing
rapidly to become an important centre of transport
and industry. Today one of the city's most famous
products, Coca-Cola, is sold all over the world.
With a population of almost three million, Atlanta
has one of the busiest airports in the world,
Hartsfield International.

The new Centennial Olympic Park is located in
the city's downtown area. The specially built
Olympic Stadium is the main focus of the Games,
with many sports being held in nearby facilities and
others some distance away. There is an Aquatic
Center for swimming and other water sports,
special hockey and soccer arenas, the Atlanta-
Fulton Stadium for baseball, a velodrome, tennis
park and many other venues.

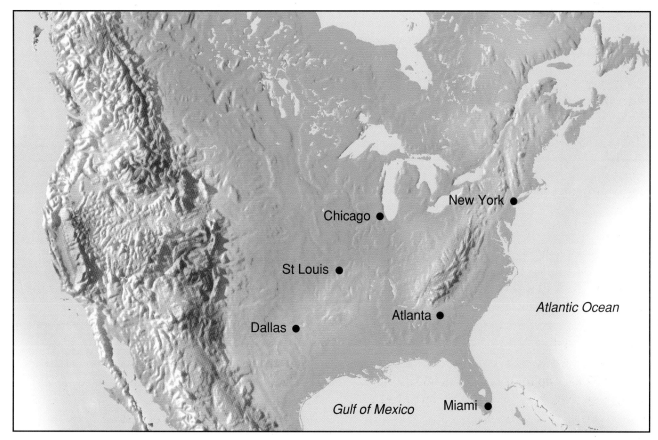

Men's sprints

IN THE ANCIENT Olympics, the sprint was the most important event. In fact for the first 13 Olympic Games it was the only event! In 1996, the sprint races are still thought by many people to be the most exciting of all the Olympic events. The winner of the 100 metres sprint can rightly be called "the fastest man in the world!"

There are three sprint races: the 100 metres, the 200 metres and the 400 metres. The running track is 400 metres in circumference, so the longest sprint is exactly one lap of the track. The 200-metre race uses half the circuit, and the 100 metres is run along the home straight. The track itself is made of a super-fast, weather-resistant synthetic material that provides excellent grip.

In the two longer sprint races, the starting lines are staggered so that the runner in the inside lane starts furthest back. The stagger is calculated so that all the athletes run exactly the same distance. Each competition starts with heats, or qualifying rounds, with eight runners reaching the final. In all races each sprinter can make one false start. If he starts too early a second time, he is disqualified.

STAR PROFILE

MICHAEL JOHNSON...

Born: Sept. 13, 1967, Dallas, Texas
1991: 200 m world champion
1992: Olympic gold 4 x 400 m
1993: 400 m world champion
world gold 4 x 400 m
1995: 400 m world indoor record
200 and 400 m US and
world champion
world gold 4 x 400 m

RUNNING GEAR

Olympic sprinters, such as Michael Johnson of the USA (*left*), wear a national team vest. Tight-fitting clothes aid streamlining. Sprinters run on the balls of their feet, so the front of the running shoes (*below*) are spiked to grip the track.

lycra vest

lycra sprinting shorts

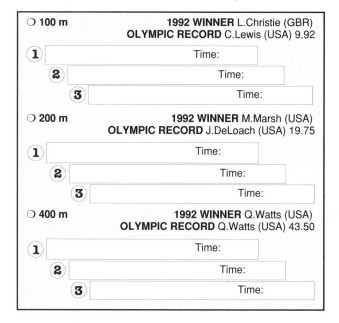

O 100 m	1992 WINNER L.Christie (GBR) OLYMPIC RECORD C.Lewis (USA) 9.92
1	Time:
2	Time:
3	Time:

O 200 m	1992 WINNER M.Marsh (USA) OLYMPIC RECORD J.DeLoach (USA) 19.75
1	Time:
2	Time:
3	Time:

O 400 m	1992 WINNER Q.Watts (USA) OLYMPIC RECORD Q.Watts (USA) 43.50
1	Time:
2	Time:
3	Time:

lightweight heel

9-mm-long spikes

ON YOUR MARKS!

In staggered races, small loudspeakers are wired to the starter's microphone and pistol (*bottom left*), so that all the runners hear his voice and the gun clearly and at the same time. Sprinters' starting blocks (*top left*) have a sensory pad to show up false starts.

QUIZ . . . .

1 Which athlete successfully defended his 100-m Olympic title in 1988?
  a) Linford Christie
  b) Carl Lewis
  c) Leroy Burrell

2 How many nations took part in the 1896 Olympic Games?
  a) 13
  b) 24
  c) 38

3 In the Olympics, what is the finishing tape made of?
  a) cotton
  b) plastic
  c) there isn't one!

Answers on page 80

PHOTO FINISH

When an athlete crosses the finishing line (*below*), he breaks a beam of light and his time is automatically recorded. A photograph records each sprinter's position and time. Here, Linford Christie is first to cross the line in the 100-m final at the 1992 Olympics.

Men's hurdles

THERE ARE two individual hurdle races for men, both over sprinting distances: the 110 metres and the 400 metres. The first is run along the straight, and the athletes have to jump 10 high hurdles. The 400 metres hurdle race is run around one lap of the track, and the hurdlers jump 10 slightly lower hurdles.

The runners must show a mixture of speed, balance and concentration. In the shorter event, one mistake can cost an athlete the race. The 400 metre hurdles is considered to be one of the most demanding races physically; athletes must run at top speed, with 10 barriers added to disrupt their rhythm.

One of the greatest 400 metre hurdlers of all time was Ed Moses of the USA. At the 1976 Olympics in Montreal he won gold in world record time, at the age of 20. He then

STAR PROFILE

DERRICK ADKINS...

Born: July 2, 1970, in New York
1987: US and Pan American Junior
     champion, 400 m hurdles
1991/93: world University Games
     champion
1993: runner-up, US Championships
     7th, World Championships
1994/95: US champion
1995: world champion

THE TECHNIQUE

A good hurdler attacks the barriers. First he lifts the lead leg (1) and extends it (2). The trail leg sweeps wide and flat over the hurdle, with the trunk leaning forward (3). Once the trail leg is over the hurdle (4), it is pulled down quickly so that the athlete gets back into his running stride as soon as possible.

went on to win 107 races in a row. This winning streak lasted nearly 10 years. He missed the 1980 Olympics, but won gold again in 1984 and bronze in 1988 at the Seoul Games. Moses' Olympic and world records were both finally broken at Barcelona in 1992, by Kevin Young, also of the USA.

PEAK OF FITNESS

The British 110 m hurdler Colin Jackson (*below*) — shown here at Edinburgh in 1994 — shows the perfect balance and fitness needed to negotiate hurdles. Certain joints take heavy stress; hurdlers need flexible hip joints, and strong thigh muscles to protect their knees.

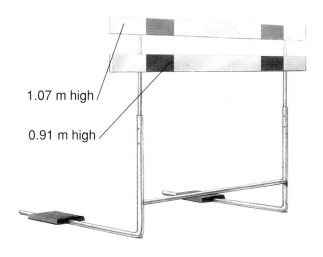

1.07 m high

0.91 m high

HIGH AND LOW HURDLES

In the men's short race, the hurdles are 1.07 m high; in the longer event they are 0.91 m high (*above*). At both distances the athletes are not disqualified if they knock over the hurdles accidentally, but it is not to their advantage to do so as it slows them down.

○ **110 m HURDLES**   **1992 WINNER** M.McKoy (Can)
OLYMPIC RECORD R.Kingdom (USA) 12.98

1 Time:
2 Time:
3 Time:

○ **400 m HURDLES**   **1992 WINNER** K.Young (USA)
OLYMPIC RECORD K.Young (USA) 46.78

1 Time:
2 Time:
3 Time:

GOING THE DISTANCE

In the short sprint hurdle, there is a distance of 9.14 m between the barriers, and in the 400 m race, the hurdles are 35 m apart, with a 40 m run-in to the finish (*below*). The great Ed Moses took 13 strides between the hurdles.

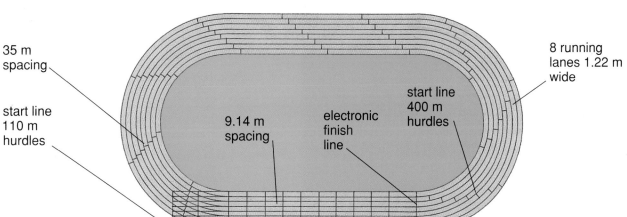

35 m spacing

start line 110 m hurdles

9.14 m spacing

electronic finish line

start line 400 m hurdles

8 running lanes 1.22 m wide

ATHLETICS track events

Men's middle distance and relays

THE MEN'S middle-distance races are run over 800 metres and 1500 metres. Both races have been part of the modern Games since the beginning. In the history of the events, only five men have won both races in the same year. This great double was last achieved 32 years ago: Peter Snell of New Zealand took both golds in 1964. The Olympic records at both distances have stood since the 1984 Los Angeles Games, and both will be under great threat in Atlanta.

The 800 metres covers two laps of the track, and the runners start in staggered lanes. They break from the lanes after the first bend. In the 1500 metres the lanes are disregarded altogether; the race is started on a curved line across the track and covers three and three-quarter laps. This is the metric equivalent of the famous mile race, and is considered to be one of the highlights of the Games. Tactics play an important part in the race, as athletes jockey for position. It is important for them to be well positioned when the bell sounds to let them know that there is one lap to go. Very often the fastest finishers keep their best efforts in reserve until the final bend.

The 4 x 400 m men's relay was introduced to the Games in 1908, and the 4 x 100 relay in 1912. The Americans have dominated both events; in 18 Olympics, they have won gold 14 times in the 4 x 100 metres, and 14 times in the 4 x 400 metres! They won both events at the last Olympics, breaking their own Olympic record and the world record at the same time!

PASSING THE BATON

The relay baton (1) is a smooth, hollow tube weighing at least 50 g. In the 4 x 100 m, the first runner in the four-man team should obviously be a fast starter, and must practise holding the baton at the start (2). The baton can be passed to the next runner using either an upsweep or a downsweep, as here (3), into his outstretched hand. Nowadays most runners prefer the downsweep method.

TIMING IT RIGHT

Kenyans have won the last two 800-m gold medals, and in Barcelona two Kenyans, William Tanui and Nixon Kiprotik (*above,* left and centre), were separated by just four hundredths of a second to gain gold and silver. Here they take the bend with Johnny Gray of the USA.

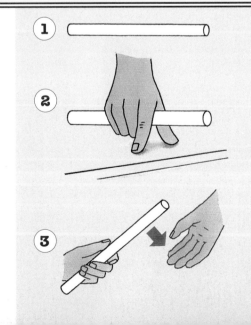

BREAKING RECORDS

Fermin Cacho Ruiz of Spain, the Olympic 1500-m champion (*left*), won the event at the 1994 European Championships too, in a championship record time. World-record times are often difficult to achieve in Olympic middle and long distance races, since everyone is genuinely racing and there are no pace-makers to set the right time in each lap.

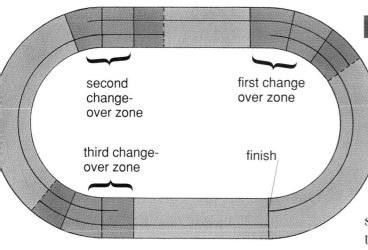

second change-over zone

first change over zone

third change-over zone

finish

CHANGE-OVER ZONES

For handing over the baton in the short-sprint relay, there are three change-over zones (*left*), each 20 m long. The baton must be passed within this area, and the runner receiving the baton may start running up to 10 m before the change-over zone. This is called the acceleration zone. Short-sprint relay runners aim to hand over the baton as close to full speed as possible. The runner receiving the baton must start at just the right moment. In Barcelona, the team from the USA finished over half a second ahead of the Nigerians to win gold.

TEAM SPIRIT

The American team is used to winning the 4 x 400 m, but in Barcelona the team was also celebrating a new world record! Here the exhausted runners enjoy their victory (*below*). Change-overs at the end of each lap can be hectic, and the runners have to concentrate hard to keep out of each other's way.

○ 800 m	1992 WINNER W.Tanui (KEN)
	OLYMPIC RECORD J.Cruz (BRA) 1:43.00
1	Time:
2	Time:
3	Time:

○ 1500 m	1992 WINNER F.Cacho Ruiz (ESP)
	OLYMPIC RECORD S.Coe (GBR) 3:32.53
1	Time:
2	Time:
3	Time:

○ 4 x 100 m RELAY	1992 WINNER USA
	OLYMPIC RECORD USA 37.40
1	Time:
2	Time:
3	Time:

○ 4 x 400 m RELAY	1992 WINNER USA
	OLYMPIC RECORD USA 2:55.74
1	Time:
2	Time:
3	Time:

ATHLETICS track events

Men's long distance

THE OLDEST of the long-distance running races is also the longest: the marathon. This supreme test of endurance was not run at Olympia, but it does have its origins in ancient Greece. In 490 BC, the Athenians defeated an army of invading Persians at a place called Marathon, northeast of Athens. Pheidippides, a champion Greek runner, ran across the hills and valleys to give the news to the people of Athens. As he gasped out the story of victory, he died. The first modern marathon race, run in honour of this ancient event, was held in Athens at the 1896 Olympics.

REFRESHMENT STATIONS

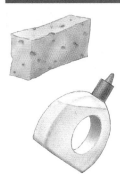

Marathon runners are given refreshment in easy-to-handle plastic bottles (*bottom left*) after about 11 km and again every 5 km or so. Wet sponges for wiping the head (*top left*) are provided at short intervals.

The 1896 marathon was run over 40 kilometres, roughly the distance from Marathon to Athens. It was won by a Greek shepherd, Spyridon Louis, in just under three hours. At the London Olympics of 1908, the race was extended slightly so that British royalty could watch the start take place in front of Windsor Castle. The distance to the finish at White City stadium was 42.295 kilometres, and since then this has been the official race distance. Today, it usually winds through city streets and ends up back in the Olympic stadium.

In 1912, two long track races, the 5000 and 10000 metres, were introduced. The distance of the steeplechase, a race over hurdles and a water jump, was standardized in 1920 at 3000 metres. There are also two road-walking races, the longer one being 50 kilometres. Imagine walking all that way — the equivalent of 125 laps of the running track — in under four hours!

BARCELONA MARATHON

Hwang Young-Cho of South Korea (*above*) ended the 1992 Olympic marathon 22 seconds ahead of Koichi Morishita of Japan. This might sound a lot, but not after 42 kilometres!

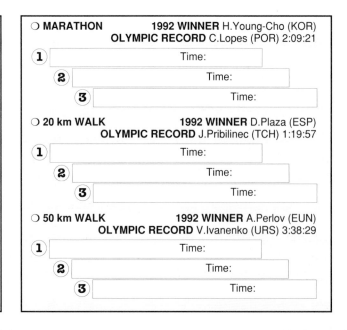

○ 5000 m	1992 WINNER D.Baumann (GER)
	OLYMPIC RECORD S.Aouita (MAR) 13:05.59
1	Time:
2	Time:
3	Time:

○ 10000 m	1992 WINNER K.Skah (MAR)
	OLYMPIC RECORD B.Boutayeb (MAR) 27:21.46
1	Time:
2	Time:
3	Time:

○ 3000 m STEEPLECHASE	1992 WINNER M.Birir (KEN)
	OLYMPIC RECORD J.Kariuki (KEN) 8:05.51
1	Time:
2	Time:
3	Time:

○ MARATHON	1992 WINNER H.Young-Cho (KOR)
	OLYMPIC RECORD C.Lopes (POR) 2:09:21
1	Time:
2	Time:
3	Time:

○ 20 km WALK	1992 WINNER D.Plaza (ESP)
	OLYMPIC RECORD J.Pribilinec (TCH) 1:19:57
1	Time:
2	Time:
3	Time:

○ 50 km WALK	1992 WINNER A.Perlov (EUN)
	OLYMPIC RECORD V.Ivanenko (URS) 3:38:29
1	Time:
2	Time:
3	Time:

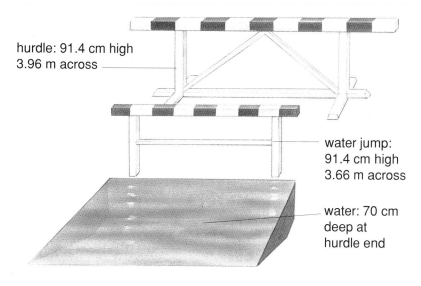

hurdle: 91.4 cm high
3.96 m across

water jump:
91.4 cm high
3.66 m across

water: 70 cm
deep at
hurdle end

STEEPLECHASE COURSE

The 3000-m steeplechase is run on the 400 m track, and there are five obstacles. At the top bend there are special lanes to include the water jump (*bottom left*). Steeplechasers usually tread on the hurdle before jumping into the water. They hurdle straight over the other four barriers (*top left*), which are solid and do not topple over.

TAKING THE PLUNGE

Steeplechasers pace their run-up to the water jump so that they take off about 1.5 m before the hurdle (*right*). After landing in the water, they try to settle back into a running rhythm as quickly as possible.

PROTEST AND APPEAL

Khalid Skah of Morocco (*left*) won the 10000 m race in Barcelona in controversial circumstances. The Kenyan team protested that Skah had impeded Richard Chelimo as he tried to step up the pace. At the same time, an official had run on to the track to push aside a lapped runner. At first Skah was disqualified, but his gold medal was returned after a Moroccan appeal.

DID YOU KNOW?

● The shepherd who won the first marathon was presented with a horse and cart for his village as well as a gold medal.

● In 1932, steeplechaser Volmari Iso-Hollo of Finland ran an extra lap by mistake, but he still won the gold medal.

● In the history of the event, only two marathon champions have successfully defended their Olympic title four years later.

THE LONG HOT WALK

The 50-km walkers will be hoping it is not too hot in Atlanta. Here Andrej Chylinski of the USA (*left*) cools off at the 1993 Monterrey championships.

Women's sprints

THE SHORT sprint, or 100-metre dash, was one of the first women's athletics events; it was introduced in 1928. Only one woman has ever successfully defended her 100-metre title at the following Games: Wyomia Tyus of the USA won in 1964 and 1968.

The women's 200 metres was first run in 1948, and for that and the next three Olympics it was won by the 100-metre winner. In 1948, some thought Fanny Blankers-Koen of the Netherlands was too old, at 30, to be in the Dutch team. Proving them wrong, she won the 100 metres, 200 metres, 80 metres hurdles and 4 x 100 metre relay. And she wasn't even allowed to compete in her strongest event, the long jump!

The most recent double-winner was Florence Griffith-Joyner of the USA, popularly known as "Flo-Jo", who in 1988 won both races in Olympic record times. Her time of 10.54 in the 100-metre final did not count in the record books, since the wind was over the allowed limit. But Flo-Jo's time of 10.62 in the quarter-final round still stands as the record.

In 1964 the 400 metres was introduced. Only one woman has ever won both the 200 and 400 metres: Valerie Brisco-Hooks of the USA in 1984. In recent years, sprinters have tended to concentrate on one event. This is partly because of the specialized training required for each event, and also because athletes prefer not to put themselves through too many qualifying rounds in a short space of time.

STAR PROFILE

MARIE-JOSÉ PÉREC...
Born: May 9, 1968, in Guadeloupe
1989: European indoor 400-m champion
1991/95: world champion
1992: Olympic champion
1994: European champion
1995: takes up 400 m hurdles

FASTEST WOMAN IN THE WORLD

As Olympic 100-m champion, Gail Devers of the USA achieved the title of "fastest woman in the world" in 1992, just a year after recovering from a serious illness. It was a brilliant final; only six hundredths of a second separated the first five runners (*right*).

SPRINT START

When the starter gives the command "On your marks!", the sprinter crouches, puts her feet on the starting blocks and kneels on her back leg (1). At "Set!", she raises her hips and is poised to start (2). When the starting gun is fired, she pushes off hard with her feet, uses a lot of arm action and tries to get into her running and reach top speed as quickly as possible (3).

ROUND THE BEND

The first half of the 200 m sprint is run around a bend, so the athletes — led here by Gwen Torrence of the USA in 1992 — must practise keeping their pace and rhythm while turning left (*above*). The inside runners have a tighter curve, but also have the advantage of being able to see the other competitors.

○ 100 m   **1992 WINNER** G.Devers (USA)
      OLYMPIC RECORD F.Griffith-Joyner (USA) 10.62

1   Time:

2   Time:

3   Time:

○ 200 m   **1992 WINNER** G.Torrence (USA)
      OLYMPIC RECORD F.Griffith-Joyner (USA) 21.34

1   Time:

2   Time:

3   Time:

○ 400 m   **1992 WINNER** M-J.Pérec
      OLYMPIC RECORD O.Bryzgina (URS) 48.65

1   Time:

2   Time:

3   Time:

LONGEST SPRINT

You could say that the 400 m is the toughest running race of all, since it is the longest sprint and the athletes run more or less flat out the whole way. Marie-José Pérec of France won gold at Barcelona (*left*), and in the European Championships in 1994 she started well and finished first, completing her set of titles — European, world and Olympic champion. She retained the world title in 1995.

Women's hurdles

THE FIRST Olympic hurdling event for women was introduced in 1932. It was the short-sprint hurdle race, run over 80 metres. Down the years there have been many famous winners, including Shirley Strickland of Australia, the only woman ever to have won hurdling gold in two successive Olympics (1952 and 1956). Paraskevi Patoulidou of Greece and Britain's Sally Gunnell will be trying to do the same in Atlanta.

At the Munich Games in 1972 the short hurdle race was lengthened to 100 metres, and it has remained so ever since. As in all hurdle races, there are 10 barriers, each 83.8 centimetres high. The hurdles are 8.5 metres apart, and the hurdlers take three strides between them. After the last hurdle, there is a run-in to the line of 10.5 metres. No woman has ever won both the 100 metres flat and the 100 metres hurdles at the Olympic Games.

The longer hurdles race, the 400 metres, was introduced for women in 1984. The hurdles are in the same position as the equivalent men's race, but are less high — 76.2 centimetres, which is also lower than the women's short-sprint hurdles. As with the men's 400-metre hurdle race, this demanding event requires great technique as well as strength, speed and stamina.

○ 100 m HURDLES	1992 WINNER P.Patoulidou (GRE)
	OLYMPIC RECORD Y.Donkova (BUL) 12.38

1	Time:
2	Time:
3	Time:

○ 400 m HURDLES	1992 WINNER S.Gunnell (GBR)
	OLYMPIC RECORD D.Flintoff-King (AUS) 53.17

1	Time:
2	Time:
3	Time:

SPEED AND TECHNIQUE

Sprint hurdle races are often won by fractions of a second. In Barcelona, Paraskevi Patoulidou (*left*, on the left) became the first Greek woman athlete to win an Olympic gold medal. She stopped the electronic clock five hundredths of a second before La Vonna Martin of the USA.

HURDLING EXERCISES

Hurdlers do special exercises to help increase their suppleness. These should only be attempted when the athlete is fully warmed-up. They include ground hurdling, or trying to touch the knee with the chest (1); the split position, or trying to touch the shin with the chin (2); a bending exercise, standing with one leg resting on a hurdle and touching the ground (3); and leg swinging, or trying to kick as high as possible in front and behind (4).

DID YOU KNOW ?

● Hurdles are designed so that a force of 3.6 to 4.0 kg applied to the middle of the crossbar will overturn them.

● A hurdler is disqualified if she trails a foot to the side of a hurdle below the level of the top.

● In the 100-m hurdles, the athletes run 13 m to the first hurdle; in the 400 m hurdles, the distance is 45 m.

● The Olympic record for 80 m hurdles was 10.39 seconds, set by Maureen Caird of Australia in the last final of 1968.

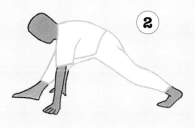

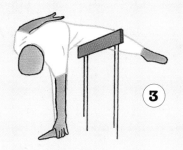

SPEED AND SKILL

Olympic 400-m champion Sally Gunnell of Britain (*left*) started her career over the higher, short-sprint hurdles. This helped her develop her superb technique. An athlete who is able to keep her rhythm over the hurdles is at a great advantage over her rivals.

SPECTACULAR STUMBLE

In the 1992 100-m hurdle final, Gail Devers of the USA looked as if she would become the first woman to win both short sprints. She had won the 100-m flat race five days earlier. But she hit the last hurdle and almost fell over the line in fifth place (*below*).

Women's middle distance and relays

WHEN WOMEN first ran on the Olympic track, at the Amsterdam Games of 1928, the 800 metres middle-distance race was one of the events included — despite opposition from Baron de Coubertin, the founder of the modern Games, and many of the world's leading sportsmen. They considered the distance to be dangerously long for women, and indeed several of the runners collapsed during the race, while others were clearly in distress.

The race was won by 17-year-old Lina Radke of Germany, in a world-record time of 2:16.80. This was Germany's first ever gold in either a track or field event; Radke's male compatriots had yet to win one.

But a ban on the race was imposed nevertheless, and it lasted for 32 years. When the race was reintroduced in 1960, it was won by Lyudmila Shevtsova of the Soviet Union, who took 12 seconds off Radke's time. The current Olympic record (a further 11 seconds less) was set in 1980. Will an even faster time be run in Atlanta?

The 1500 metres was introduced in 1972, when it took over as the longest women's race. This lasted until 1984, when the women's marathon was included in the Games. Many women have competed in both the 800 metres and 1500 metres, but only one woman has ever won at both distances in the Olympics. Tatyana Kazankina of the Soviet Union took both golds in 1976, and she won the 1500 metres again in 1980.

The 4 x 100 metres short relay was also one of the first women's track events; it too was first held in 1928. In recent Games the event has been dominated by the USA, who have won the last three Olympic golds. The 4 x 400 metres long relay was introduced in 1972; both relays are now well established as final-day women's Olympic track events.

FLYING WINGER

When she was 22, Ellen van Langen of the Netherlands was playing on the wing for a Dutch women's soccer team. Four years later, in Barcelona, she won gold in the 800 m (*left*). Her burst of speed in the final sprint must have made many soccer full-backs hope she would stick to athletics from then on!

800 m	1992 WINNER E.van Langen (NED)
	OLYMPIC RECORD N.Olizarenko (URS) 1:53.43
1	Time:
2	Time:
3	Time:

1500 m	1992 WINNER H.Boulmerka (ALG)
	OLYMPIC RECORD P.Ivan (ROM) 3:53.96
1	Time:
2	Time:
3	Time:

4 x 100 m RELAY	1992 WINNER USA
	OLYMPIC RECORD GDR 41.60
1	Time:
2	Time:
3	Time:

4 x 400 m RELAY	1992 WINNER EUN
	OLYMPIC RECORD URS 3:15.18
1	Time:
2	Time:
3	Time:

OLYMPIC AND WORLD CHAMPION

Hassiba Boulmerka gained Algeria's first ever track gold medal in Barcelona, winning the 1500 m in fine style (*right*). She is also the current world champion, having beaten Britain's Kelly Holmes into second place in Gothenburg in 1995. Boulmerka always shows tremendous strength and stamina in her running.

RELAY QUEEN

At the last Olympics, Gwen Torrence of the USA (*below*) led her team home to gold in the 4 x 100 m relay. She was also in the silver-winning 4 x 400 m team. Torrence was born in Atlanta, and will be particularly keen to repeat her medal-winning performances in front of a home crowd.

CHANGE-OVER

Baton change-overs in relays must be smooth. If a competitor drops the baton, she must pick it up before continuing. Here, Britain's Stephanie Llewellyn (*right, on the right*) passes the baton to Melanie Neef in the 4 x 400 m relay in the 1995 World Championships. From a slow start, there is less chance of dropping the baton.

19

Women's long distance |||||

UNTIL 1972, the longest distance run by Olympic women was 1500 metres. Then in 1984 the 3000 metres and the marathon race were both introduced. This was a breakthrough for female long-distance runners, and they have not looked back since. At the Atlanta Games, a 5000-metre race will replace the 3000 metres, which means that training patterns and distances have changed for many of the competitors. The 10000 metres was first run in Seoul in 1988, and was won by Olga Bondarenko of the then Soviet Union. Four years later the title of

10000-metre champion went to 20-year-old Derartu Tulu of Ethiopia, the first Ethiopian woman to win an Olympic gold in any athletics event. She beat Elana Meyer of South Africa by over five seconds.

In recent years, more and more women athletes have devoted themselves to the marathon, a 42.295 kilometre road race run through city streets. The time run by Joan Benoit of the USA in Los Angeles in 1984 — two hours, 24 minutes and 52 seconds — remains the Olympic record, though marathon records are considered unofficial because each course is so different from the last in terms of surface and circuit. A record nine women ran under two hours and 30 minutes in 1984.

The first women's 10-kilometre walk was introduced to the Games in Barcelona. In this event, the athletes must have one foot in contact with the ground at all times.

LAST EVER OLYMPIC 3000?

Barcelona's 3000 metres race has been replaced by Atlanta's 5000 metres. In 1992, Sonia O'Sullivan of Ireland (*left*) missed a medal by just two tenths of a second. Two years later, she won gold at the European championships in a much faster time.

○ **5000 m**   **NEW EVENT**
1 | Time:
2 | Time:
3 | Time:

○ **10000 m**   **1992 WINNER** D.Tulu (ETH)
OLYMPIC RECORD O.Bondarenko (URS) 31:05.21
1 | Time:
2 | Time:
3 | Time:

○ **MARATHON**   **1992 WINNER** V.Yegorova (EUN)
OLYMPIC RECORD J.Benoit (USA) 2:24:52
1 | Time:
2 | Time:
3 | Time:

○ **10 km WALK**   **1992 WINNER** C.Yueling (CHN)
OLYMPIC RECORD C.Yueling (CHN) 44:32
1 | Time:
2 | Time:
3 | Time:

QUIZ . . . .

1 Who won the women's 10000 metres 1994 World Cup race in London?
   a) Sonia O'Sullivan
   b) Elana Meyer
   c) Liz McColgan

2 Is the women's marathon longer or shorter than the men's?
   a) longer
   b) shorter
   c) same distance

3 Atlanta is the capital of which US state?
   a) Georgia
   b) Florida
   c) it's not a state capital

Answers on page 80

AFRICAN ONE AND TWO

Derartu Tulu of Ethiopia (*above*, left) and Elana Meyer of South Africa (*above*, right) enjoyed their lap of honour together after the 10000 metres in Barcelona. A united Africa was the sporting winner. South Africa was back in the Olympics after being excluded for 32 years due to its former policy of apartheid.

WALKING TECHNIQUE

Surely you don't need great athletic skill to walk, you may think. But it's not so easy when you are trying to walk very fast, without ever losing contact with the ground. After the leading leg hits the ground (1), it must be straightened for a moment while the foot is on the ground (2). This gives athletic walkers their characteristic rolling gait. If a competitor breaks the walking rule, she is cautioned with a white flag. If she repeats the offence, a red flag is shown, disqualifying her.

10 KM IN 44 MINUTES

The walkers stride out at the start of the 1994 European Championships in Helsinki (*below*). The event was won by Sari Essayah of Finland, who came fourth in the last Olympics.

1   **2**

The Decathlon

PEOPLE OFTEN describe the winners of the men's decathlon (meaning a 10-event contest) and the women's heptathlon (a seven-event contest) as the greatest athletes in the world. These multiple events demand great strength and stamina, as well as speed, from the competitors. The first multiple-event competition of this kind, the pentathlon, or five-event contest, was held by the ancient Greeks in 708 BC, and comprised foot racing, long jump, discus, javelin and wrestling. The present version of the decathlon was introduced to the modern Games in 1912. It was won that year by Jim Thorpe of the USA, who came first ahead of Hugo Weislander of Sweden. Thorpe was then disqualified for being a professional athlete, though he was reinstated in 1982, after his death, as joint gold-medal winner.

Included in the 10 events of the modern decathlon, which takes place over two days, are four races: the event begins with the 100-metres sprint, and ends with the 1500 metres; in between are the 400 metres and 110-metre hurdles. There are three jumping events: long jump, high jump and pole vault. And there are three throws: shot put, discus and javelin. In all 10 events, points are awarded to the athletes for achieving set times, heights and distances, rather than for their position compared to others. The competitor with most points is the champion and gold-medal winner.

DECATHLETES' SHOES

Competitors need different shoes for different events. They wear running spikes for the three sprints, and may have a slightly different pair for the 1500-m race. The spikes on long-jump shoes improve grip on the take-off board. For the high jump and pole vault, the shoes often have spikes on the heels to give good grip on the run-up. No spikes are needed for shot-put and discus shoes. High-sided javelin-throwing shoes support the ankles and have spikes on the soles and heels.

EXTRA ATTEMPT

At the Barcelona Olympic Games the judges allowed Dave Johnson of the USA a fourth attempt in the shot put (*left*). His three previous attempts had all been invalid, so he would have scored no shot-put points at all. After this controversial decision, Johnson went on to win the decathlon bronze medal.

running shoe

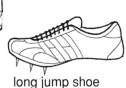

long jump shoe

high jump shoe

discus shoe

javelin shoe

THREE ATTEMPTS

In the throws and jumps, each decathlete is allowed just three attempts. Here, Dezso Szabo of Hungary (*left*) attempts to improve his distance in the discus throwing on day two of the decathlon.

DECIDING RACE

Since the 1500 m race is the final event in the decathlon, the athletes usually know what sort of time they must achieve in order to win overall. Current Olympic champion Robert Zmelik of the Czech Republic (*below*) used the 1500 m to boost his points total to 8611. This was 236 points short of the Olympic record held by British athlete Daley Thompson, who won gold in 1980 and 1984.

DECATHLON PROGRAMME

How many of the 10 events will the 1996 Olympic gold-medallist win? The table (*below*) shows the events in order. Fill in the winners over two days, but remember, it is the overall points that really count for the three medals.

EVENT	WINNER	POINTS
DAY 1		
100 m		
LONG JUMP		
SHOT PUT		
HIGH JUMP		
400 m		
DAY 2		
110 m HURDLES		
DISCUS		
POLE VAULT		
JAVELIN		
1500 m		

○ DECATHLON	1992 **WINNER** R.Zmelik (TCH)
	OLYMPIC RECORD D.Thompson (GBR) 8847

1 _____ Points: _____

2 _____ Points: _____

3 _____ Points: _____

ATHLETICS

The Heptathlon

THE ATHLETIC multiple event for women started in 1964 as the five-part pentathlon. Twenty years later, two further parts were added, so in the last three Olympics women have competed in the "heptathlon" (a Greek word meaning a seven-part contest). The winning heptathlete can rightly say she is the finest all-round athlete.

The heptathlon's seven events are held over two days, just like the men's decathlon. The competition begins with the 100-metre hurdles and ends with the 800-metre race; there is also a 200-metre race in the middle. There are two jumping events, the high jump and long jump, as well as two throws, the shot put and javelin. As with the decathlon, the winner is the athlete who gains the most points overall.

At the 1984 Los Angeles Olympics, the first-ever heptathlon was won by Glynis Nunn of Australia, who beat Jackie Joyner-Kersee of the USA by just five points. Four years later, in Seoul, Jackie Joyner-Kersee added an amazing 904 points to break the world record, Olympic record and win the gold medal. At the next Olympiad, in Barcelona, she again showed her brilliance by retaining her top position.

STAR PROFILE

JACKIE JOYNER-KERSEE...
Born: March 3, 1962, in East St Louis, USA
1976: US junior pentathlon champion
1984: Olympic heptathlon silver
1986/88: breaks world record four times
1987: world champion
1988: Olympic champion, heptathlon and long jump
1992: Olympic champion, heptathlon

EVENT	WINNER	POINTS
DAY 1		
100 m HURDLES		
HIGH JUMP		
SHOT PUT		
200 m		
DAY 2		
LONG JUMP		
JAVELIN		
800 m		

HEPTATHLON PROGRAMME

How many of the seven events will the 1996 Olympic gold-medallist win? The table (*above*) shows the events in order, so you can fill in the winners over two days. But remember, as with the men's decathlon, it is the overall points that really count for the three medals.

EUROPEAN CHAMPION

Sabine Braun of Germany jumped a personal best height of 1.94 m in the 1992 heptathlon high jump (*above*), and took the bronze medal. She was already European champion, and she retained that title in 1994.

JJ-K ON DAY TWO

In Barcelona, Jackie Joyner-Kersee (*right*) not only took gold in the heptathlon for a second time; she also won long jump bronze in the women's jumping events. Here she lands in the sand on day two of the heptathlon.

| ○ HEPTATHLON | 1992 WINNER J.Joyner-Kersee (USA) |
| OLYMPIC RECORD J.Joyner-Kersee (USA) 7291 |

1 _____ Points: _____
2 _____ Points: _____
3 _____ Points: _____

THE FINAL TEST

The 800 m race is the last event of the two-day contest, and the heptathletes are already tired when they are faced with this challenge. In the 1993 world championships, the heptathlon 800-m race was won by Beatrice Mau of Germany (*below*, right).

QUIZ . . . .

1 How many heptathlon events are also in the decathlon?
   a) 2
   b) 3
   c) 4

2 Who is Jackie Joyner-Kersee's famous sprinting sister-in-law?
   a) Evelyn Ashford
   b) Florence Griffith-Joyner
   c) Gail Devers

3 How many attempts does a heptathlete have in each jumping event?
   a) 3
   b) 4
   c) 6

Answers on page 80

Men's jumping

THE FOUR MEN'S jumping events are the long jump, high jump, triple jump and pole vault. All were included in the 1896 Games. In the past many sprinters competed in the long jump too. Today, the jumpers tend to be specialists in one event. In the long jump, a leap is measured from the take-off board to the nearest mark made in the sandpit by any part of the body. If an athlete leaves an impression in the strip of soft modelling material just in front of the take-off board, a red flag is raised to show a "no jump". The same rules apply to the triple jump, but in this event the athlete must make a hop and a step before he jumps.

High jumpers must take off on one foot. They get greatest height by jumping backwards — a technique introduced in 1968 by Dick Fosbury of the USA. Before this, athletes straddled or rolled over the bar and landed on their fronts.

Pole vaulting has also changed; the pole was originally made of wood, then bamboo, and in the 1950s aluminium was used. Then came the light, bendy fibreglass poles used today.

THE FOSBURY FLOP

In 1968, Dick Fosbury won gold with a sensational new technique. Instead of swinging a leg over the bar and landing face down, he ran at the bar and jumped backwards.

LEAP OF THE CENTURY

At Mexico City in 1968, Bob Beamon of the USA made the greatest long jump in Olympic history (*above*). At 8.90 m, his jump added 78 cm to the Olympic record and shattered the world record too. This amazing Olympic record still stands.

UP ON FOSBURY

At Barcelona in 1992, Javier Sotomayor of Cuba (*right*) won the gold medal in the high jump using Fosbury's technique. He added a remarkable 10 cm to Fosbury's height of 2.24 m.

○ LONG JUMP	**1992 WINNER** C.Lewis (USA)
OLYMPIC RECORD B.Beamon (USA) 8.90	

①	Distance:
②	Distance:
③	Distance:

○ TRIPLE JUMP	**1992 WINNER** M.Conley (USA)
OLYMPIC RECORD M.Conley (USA) 18.17	

①	Distance:
②	Distance:
③	Distance:

○ HIGH JUMP	**1992 WINNER** J.Sotomayor (CUB)
OLYMPIC RECORD G.Avdeyenko (URS) 2.38	

①	Height:
②	Height:
③	Height:

○ POLE VAULT	**1992 WINNER** M.Tarassov (EUN)
OLYMPIC RECORD S.Bubka (URS) 5.90	

①	Height:
②	Height:
③	Height:

HOP, STEP AND JUMP

In the triple jump, the athlete must first hop by landing (2) on the same foot as his take-off foot (1). Then he makes a long step onto the other foot (3), and jumps into the landing pit (4).

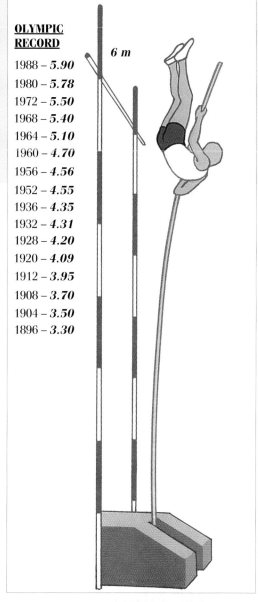

OLYMPIC RECORD

6 m

1988 – *5.90*
1980 – *5.78*
1972 – *5.50*
1968 – *5.40*
1964 – *5.10*
1960 – *4.70*
1956 – *4.56*
1952 – *4.55*
1936 – *4.35*
1932 – *4.31*
1928 – *4.20*
1920 – *4.09*
1912 – *3.95*
1908 – *3.70*
1904 – *3.50*
1896 – *3.30*

UP AND UP

The Olympic pole vault record (*left*) has gone up and up since 1896, when it started at 3.30 m. In 1988 Sergey Bubka of the then Soviet Union raised the record to 5.90 m — where it still stands — an increase of almost 80 percent on the original. Bubka, a Ukrainian, has often vaulted over 6.0 m, but in 1992 he lost the gold medal to the Russian, Maxim Tarassov.

DID YOU KNOW ?

● Until 1912 there were high jump and long jump events done from a standing start without a run-up.

● Mike Conley triple-jumped 18.17 m at Barcelona in 1992 — 56 cm further than the previous Olympic record of 17.61 m set in Seoul in 1988 by Khristo Markov of Bulgaria.

● In the high jump and pole vault, if two athletes tie by clearing the same height, the winner is the competitor with fewer earlier failures.

ATHLETICS field events

27

Men's throwing

MALE OLYMPIC athletes have four different throwing events: the discus, javelin, shot and hammer. The discus formed part of the ancient Olympics and has been a modern event since 1896. The javelin, also an ancient sport, was re-introduced in 1906. The shot has been one of the events in the Games since 1896, and the hammer since 1900. Compared with those early days, athletes now throw the discus and "put" — push away from the body, not throw — the shot over twice as far. The distances have increased almost as much with the hammer and javelin.

Shot putters and hammer throwers both use a heavy metal ball that weighs 7.26 kilograms. They throw from a circle just over 2.0 metres wide. The discus circle is 2.5 metres wide, and the discus itself weighs 2.0 kilograms. The javelin is an updated spear, with a pointed shaft and a cord grip. It weighs 800 grams. All four throws are potentially dangerous to other athletes, officials and even spectators; javelin throwers must wait for track athletes to pass the end of their throwing area before they may throw.

Qualifying rounds are held for all four events; all athletes who throw a set distance go on to the final. If fewer than 12 athletes qualify, the number in the final is made up to 12. The finalists have three throws, and the eight who throw farthest have a further three throws. The longest single throw wins gold.

STAR PROFILE

Jan Zelezny...
Born: June 16, 1966, in Mlada Boleslav, Czech Republic
1992: Olympic champion with new Olympic record
1993/95: world champion

JAVELIN GRIPS

The "Finnish" method (1) is the most popular grip among top-class throwers. The V or "claw" grip (2) is good for beginners, and a third method is the "darts" grip (3).

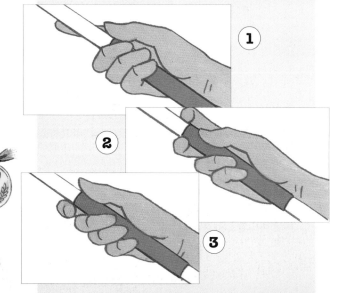

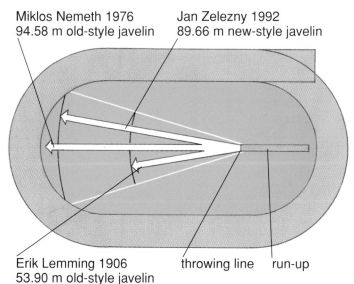

Miklos Nemeth 1976
94.58 m old-style javelin

Jan Zelezny 1992
89.66 m new-style javelin

Erik Lemming 1906
53.90 m old-style javelin

throwing line   run-up

JAVELIN RECORDS

In 1906, the javelin record was set by Erik Lemming of Sweden with a throw of 53.90 m. By 1976 Miklos Nemeth of Hungary had thrown 94.58 m. In 1986, the javelin was made less aerodynamic to reduce the distance it could be thrown, as throwers were in danger of hitting the far end of the stadium. Jan Zelezny's throw of 89.66 m (see *above*) set a new Olympic record with the new-style javelin.

PUTTING THE SHOT

There are two techniques: rotational (shown here) and linear. The athlete starts with his feet close to the circle's rim (1), then he turns around the left leg (2). The right foot moves to the centre (3), and as the left leg is brought down (4), the shot is released (5). In the linear technique, the athlete backs across the circle and half-turns to throw.

THROWING THE HAMMER

The thrower grips a triangular handle, which is attached to a wire with a heavy weight at the end. The weight resembles a ball rather than a real hammer. After swinging the hammer around and then rotating himself up to four times in the circle to gain momentum (*left*), the thrower hurls the hammer backwards, as if over his shoulder.

⬡ SHOT PUT	1992 WINNER M.Stulce (USA)
	OLYMPIC RECORD U.Timmermann (GDR) 22.47

1	Distance:
2	Distance:
3	Distance:

⬡ DISCUS	1992 WINNER R.Ubartas (LTU)
	OLYMPIC RECORD J.Schult (GDR) 68.82

1	Distance:
2	Distance:
3	Distance:

⬡ HAMMER	1992 WINNER A.Abduvaliyev (EUN)
	OLYMPIC RECORD S.Litvinov (URS) 84.80

1	Distance:
2	Distance:
3	Distance:

⬡ JAVELIN	1992 WINNER J.Zelezny (TCH)
	OLYMPIC RECORD J.Zelezny (TCH) 89.66

1	Distance:
2	Distance:
3	Distance:

DID YOU KNOW ?

● The ancient Greeks used a bronze plate for their discus.

● In the ancient Olympics, the javelin was thrown not only for distance, but also for accuracy.

● The discus is the only athletics event in which a world record has never been set in the Olympics.

● Al Oerter (USA) won four consecutive discus golds between 1956 and 1968; each winning throw was a new Olympic record.

Women's jumping

WOMEN ATHLETES first took part in the modern Olympics at the 1928 Amsterdam Games. There was only one jumping event: the high jump, won by Ethel Catherwood of Canada who jumped 1.59 metres. Four years later, in Los Angeles, Jean Shiley and Mildred Didrikson of the USA both jumped six centimetres higher. Didrikson could have been disqualified for jumping head-first over the bar, but the judges illogically awarded her the silver medal! She also won gold in the javelin and 80-metre hurdles events. In 1992, the highest jump was 2.02 metres—43 centimetres higher than Catherwood's 1928 jump.

The women's long jump first appeared in 1948 and, like the high jump, has been part of the Olympics ever since. In the Tokyo Games of

LANDING

In both long jump and triple jump, each jump is measured from the edge of the take-off board to the first break in the sand made by any part of the jumper's body. This might be the elbow (1) or the bottom (2), if the athlete sits back after landing (3). Athletes use different techniques to gain as much distance as possible.

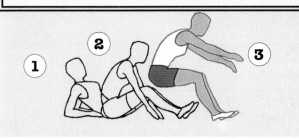

1964, the British athlete Mary Rand leapt 6.76 metres, breaking the Olympic and world long-jump records. She was the first British woman to win gold in Olympic track and field events.

The women's triple jump is a new event in 1996. Which nation will win the new gold medal?

○ HIGH JUMP	1992 WINNER H.Henkel (GER)
	OLYMPIC RECORD L.Ritter (USA) 2.03
1	Height:
2	Height:
3	Height:

○ LONG JUMP	1992 WINNER H.Drechsler (GER)
	OLYMPIC RECORD J.Joyner-Kersee (USA) 7.40
1	Distance:
2	Distance:
3	Distance:

○ TRIPLE JUMP	NEW EVENT
1	Distance:
2	Distance:
3	Distance:

HANGING IN THE AIR

After take-off (1), long jumpers extend their bodies (2) so that they can hang in the air longer. The athletes' arms move in a circle, helping their balance before landing (3). Some move their legs as if they are cycling in the air, a technique known as the hitch-kick.

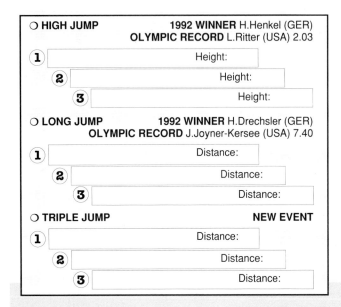

From 1968 to 1988 two German teams took part in the Olympics, the Federal Republic (West) and the Democratic Republic (East). Germany then reunified, and in the 1992 Olympics the country was represented by a single team that dominated the women's field events. Heike Henkel (*below*) won the high jump and Heike Drechsler the long jump.

TURNING THE TABLES

In Barcelona gold-medallist Heike Drechsler (*right*) turned the tables on bronze-medallist Jackie Joyner-Kersee of the USA in the long jump. Four years earlier, in Seoul, Joyner-Kersee had beaten Drechsler into second place.

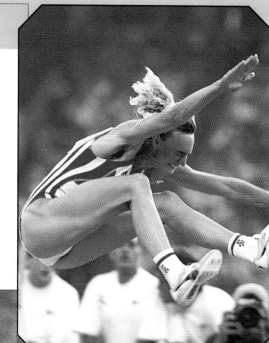

A FIRST IN 1996!

The triple jump is new to many women's athletics meetings. It formed part of the European Championships in 1994, when the event was won by Ana Biryukova of Russia (seen here *left* in 1993). Her hop, step and jump reached 14.89 m. Can she repeat the winning performance in Atlanta?

Women's throwing

THE DISCUS was the first of the women's throwing events to be part of the Olympic Games; it was introduced in 1928. Four years later the javelin made its appearance, and the women's shot was finally introduced in 1948. All three events proved very popular and have been part of every Games since their introduction. The women's throwing implements are like the men's in design, but are lighter.

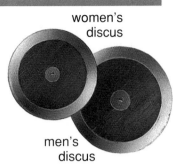

women's discus

women's javelin

men's discus

men's shot

men's javelin

women's shot

EQUIPMENT COMPARISON

The women's discus weighs 1 kg, the men's 2 kg; the women's javelin 600 g, the men's 800 g; and the women's shot 4 kg, the men's 7.26 kg.

THROWING THE DISCUS

The discus is thrown from a circle 2.5 m wide. There are no special rules about the way in which the throw must be made. All athletes use the sling method because this gives an aerodynamic throw that makes the discus travel furthest. To start, the thrower holds the discus at shoulder height (1) and swings the discus across her body from behind (2). She then spins across the circle (3), and after one and a half turns (4), she extends her throwing arm (5) and releases the discus in an easy and balanced manner (6). A discus thrower is disqualified if she steps out of the circle.

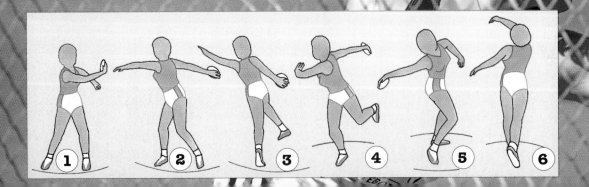

(1) (2) (3) (4) (5) (6)

GERMAN GOLD

A javelin thrower takes a run-up to make sure that the javelin is launched at the greatest possible speed, and she releases it as high above the ground as possible, usually at an angle lower than 45°. Back in 1932, Mildred Didrikson of the USA won the event with a throw of 43.68 m. Since then the winning distance has steadily increased, and in 1992 Silke Renk of Germany covered a distance of 68.34 m with her last throw (*above*). This was 8 cm further than Natalya Shikolenko of the Unified Team.

PUTTING THE SHOT

In the 1995 athletics world championships at Gothenburg, Astrid Kumbernuss of Germany (*below*) threw the winning shot put, taking the title from Zhi-hong Huang of China. Huang also won silver in the 1992 Olympics, throwing over half a metre less than Svetlana Kriveleva of the Unified Team. The Olympic record of 22.41 m has stood since 1980, when it was set by Ilona Slupianek of East Germany.

A T H L E T I C S field events

QUIZ . . . .

1 Which country has won most gold medals for women's throwing events?
   a) USA
   b) the former Soviet Union
   c) Romania

2 Lia Manoliu (ROM) won the discus in 1968 to become the oldest female Olympic champion. How old do you think she was?
   a) 36
   b) 40
   c) 44

3 In which throwing event do competitors wear spikes?
   a) shot
   b) discus
   c) javelin

Answers on page 80

○ **DISCUS**   **1992 WINNER** M.Marten (CUB)
     OLYMPIC RECORD M.Hellmann (GDR) 72.30

1   Distance:
    2   Distance:
      3   Distance:

○ **JAVELIN**   **1992 WINNER** S.Renk (GER)
     OLYMPIC RECORD P.Felke (GDR) 74.68

1   Distance:
    2   Distance:
      3   Distance:

○ **SHOT PUT**   **1992 WINNER** S.Kriveleva (EUN)
     OLYMPIC RECORD I.Slupianek (GDR) 22.41

1   Distance:
    2   Distance:
      3   Distance:

THE BACK~UP TEAM

MANY SPECTATORS and home television viewers of the Olympics would be amazed at the amount of work that goes on behind the scenes in each of the 26 separate Olympic sports. All the competitors need a large back-up team to help them prepare for the big day. In many sports, such as athletics, members of the back-up team have only the competitors to worry about. But in the equestrian events, there are also animals to look after and a great deal of equipment to transport.

Each national equestrian squad takes its own horses, as well as a large back-up team to look after the animals. A national team such as Great Britain or Germany may take as many as 20 horses to cover the three disciplines: show jumping, dressage and the three-day event. The team includes a reserve rider, one trainer for each of the three disciplines, a groom for each of the horses, vets and a farrier to replace horseshoes.

The team sends out in advance about five tonnes of freight, which includes all the new equipment from the various sponsors of the team, as well as the official Olympic uniform (boots, breeches and jackets for the riders, and saddles, bridles and rugs for the horses). Spare rugs, bandages and grooming tools are also sent ahead. In addition, a small trunk travels out with the horses, containing hay for the flight, any special feeds needed by individual horses, and a first-aid kit for minor cuts or bruises.

GOOD GROOMING

Olympic horses generally have their own groom (*below*) as well as their own rider, so there may be up to 20 grooms in a team. The grooms do a most important job. As well as feeding and caring for their horse, they exercise it and then prepare it for each event. This may involve brushing the coat, and then clipping, trimming and plaiting the mane and tail. After a ride, the horses need a full groom and brush down.

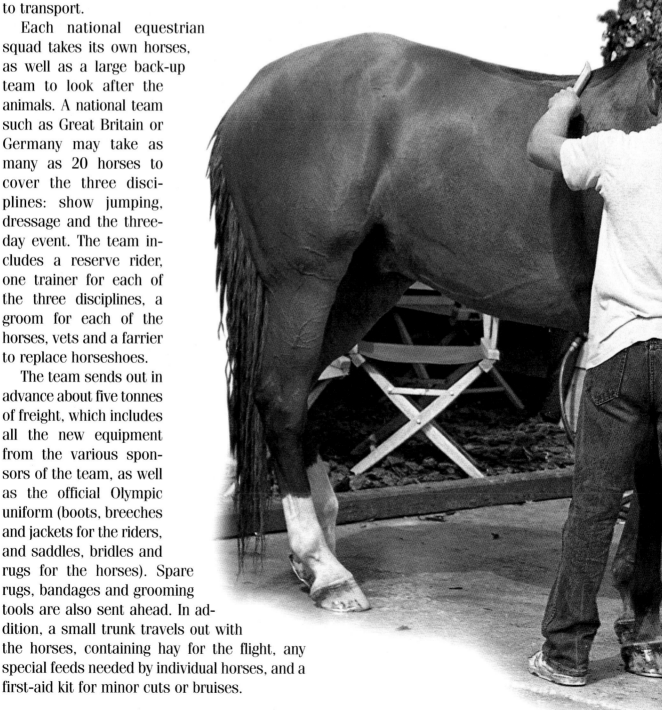

CROSS-COUNTRY BOOTS

To protect their legs in the cross-country, the horses may wear boots underneath exercise bandages, which are sewn up for extra security (*below*).

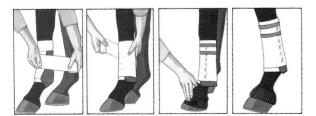

SADDLES

Different saddles are used for the three events, and many riders take spares. All the leather equipment is polished to keep it supple (*below*).

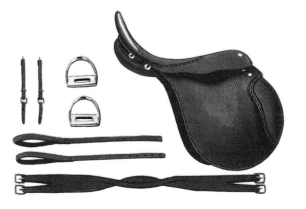

ESSENTIAL EQUIPMENT

The riders take a range of different bridles, bits — the metal mouthpiece — and other tack (*below, right*) for their horses. The tack varies according to the particular discipline. In the three-day event competition, most horses have metal studs (*below, left*) fitted to their shoes to provide grip. These come in various sizes. The "T"-shaped tool (the tap) threads the stud holes, and the studs are fitted with a spanner.

VETS ON HAND

The equestrian team includes a number of veterinary surgeons (or "vets"), who look after the animals (*below*). They keep a careful watch for any signs of ill health and treat any bumps or bruises. Because Atlanta has a very hot, humid climate, all the horses will be sent to Georgia at least three weeks before the Games, so they can get used to the conditions.

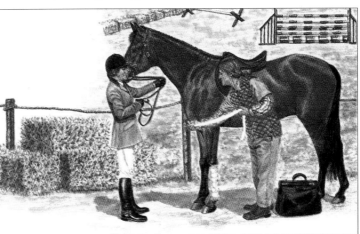

Men's events

THERE WAS no swimming in the ancient Olympics, but the sport was part of the first modern Olympics in 1896, when races were held in the sea off Piraeus, near Athens. The first Olympic race in a pool took place in 1908, in a 100-metre-long tank built inside the running track in London.

The most successful Olympic swimming nation has been the USA, followed by Australia and Germany. There are 16 men's races, and in 1992 the United States won gold in six of them. Their great rivals, the Unified Team, won five.

○ 100 m BACKSTROKE   1992 WINNER M.Tewksbury (CAN)
OLYMPIC RECORD M.Tewksbury (CAN) 53.98
1 Time:
2 Time:
3 Time:

○ 200 m BACKSTROKE 1992 WINNER M.López-Zubero (ESP)
OLYMPIC RECORD M.López-Zubero (ESP) 1:58.47
1 Time:
2 Time:
3 Time:

○ 100 m BREASTSTROKE   1992 WINNER N.Diebel (USA)
OLYMPIC RECORD N.Diebel (USA) 1:01.50
1 Time:
2 Time:
3 Time:

○ 200 m BREASTSTROKE 1992 WINNER M.Barrowman (USA)
OLYMPIC RECORD M.Barrowman (USA) 2:10.16
1 Time:
2 Time:
3 Time:

○ 50 m FREESTYLE   1992 WINNER A.Popov (EUN)
OLYMPIC RECORD A.Popov (EUN) 21.91
1 Time:
2 Time:
3 Time:

○ 100 m FREESTYLE   1992 WINNER A.Popov (EUN)
OLYMPIC RECORD M.Biondi (USA) 48.63
1 Time:
2 Time:
3 Time:

○ 200 m FREESTYLE   1992 WINNER E.Sadoviy (EUN)
OLYMPIC RECORD E.Sadoviy (EUN) 1:46.70
1 Time:
2 Time:
3 Time:

○ 400 m FREESTYLE   1992 WINNER E.Sadoviy (EUN)
OLYMPIC RECORD E.Sadoviy (EUN) 3:45.00
1 Time:
2 Time:
3 Time:

○ 1500 m FREESTYLE   1992 WINNER K.Perkins (AUS)
OLYMPIC RECORD K.Perkins (AUS) 14:43.48
1 Time:
2 Time:
3 Time:

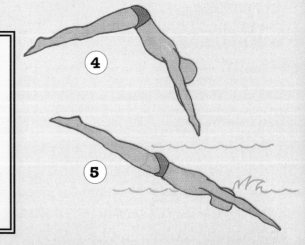

RACING START

In front crawl, breaststroke and butterfly, the swimmer starts with feet and hands on the edge of the diving block (1). He then bends his knees (2), stretches forward (3), and straightens his body, which is allowed to pike (4) to give him drive and lift. The straight body position must be regained for entry into the water (5).

BACKSTROKE START

Backstroke races begin in the water. Swimmers grasp rails on the blocks, pull themselves towards the edge of the pool and drive off hard on the starting signal (*right*). Back crawl is the fastest type of backstroke.

○ **100 m BUTTERFLY**   1992 WINNER P.Morales (USA)
OLYMPIC RECORD A.Nesty (SUR) 53.00
1 Time:
2 Time:
3 Time:

○ **200 m BUTTERFLY**   1992 WINNER M.Stewart (USA)
OLYMPIC RECORD M.Stewart (USA) 1:56.26
1 Time:
2 Time:
3 Time:

○ **200 m INDIV. MEDLEY**   1992 WINNER T.Darnyi (HUN)
OLYMPIC RECORD T.Darnyi (HUN) 2:00.17
1 Time:
2 Time:
3 Time:

○ **400 m INDIV. MEDLEY**   1992 WINNER T.Darnyi (HUN)
OLYMPIC RECORD T.Darnyi (HUN) 4:14.23
1 Time:
2 Time:
3 Time:

○ **4x100 m FREESTYLE RELAY**   1992 WINNER USA
OLYMPIC RECORD USA 3:16.53
1 Time:
2 Time:
3 Time:

○ **4x200 m FREESTYLE RELAY**   1992 WINNER EUN
OLYMPIC RECORD EUN 7:11.95
1 Time:
2 Time:
3 Time:

○ **4x100 m MEDLEY RELAY**   1992 WINNER USA
OLYMPIC RECORD USA 3:36.93
1 Time:
2 Time:
3 Time:

THE LONELINESS OF THE LONG-DISTANCE SWIMMER

Kieren Perkins of Australia (*below*) won the longest race in Barcelona, the 1500 m freestyle, in a new Olympic and world record time of 14:43.48. Perkins' average speed over 30 lengths was just 10 percent slower than the winner of the 200 m (4-length) race!

OLYMPIC AND WORLD CHAMPION

The Russian Alexandre Popov, representing the Unified Team, won the 50 m freestyle in 1992 (*above*, left); his great rival Matt Biondi of the USA (*above*, right), who won five gold medals in 1988, came in second behind the Russian. Popov also beat Biondi into fifth place in the 100 m freestyle in 1992, and went on to win both races again at the 1994 world championships in Rome.

SWIMMING

Women's events

WOMEN FIRST swam in the Olympics in 1912, when there were two freestyle events. Backstroke and breaststroke were added 12 years later, but butterfly did not come in until 1956. Today there are 17 swimming events altogether. In the medley races, all four strokes are swum.

The shortest race is just one length of the 50-metre long pool, and the longest is 16 lengths. The freestyle races are the fastest, followed by butterfly, then backstroke and finally breaststroke.

Races are timed electronically. The starting signal triggers the timing system, and sensor pads stop the clock for each swimmer as she touches the wall. After heats, the fastest qualifier swims in lane four in the final. The next quickest swims in lane five, the next in lane three, then six, two, seven, one, and the slowest in lane eight.

Six different nations won gold medals for women's swimming in 1992: China, the USA, Germany, Hungary, the Unified Team and Japan. How many will win gold in Atlanta in 1996?

○ **50 m FREESTYLE**   1992 WINNER W.Yang (CHN)
OLYMPIC RECORD W.Yang (CHN) 24.79
① Time:
② Time:
③ Time:

○ **100 m FREESTYLE**   1992 WINNER Y.Zhuang (CHN)
OLYMPIC RECORD Y.Zhuang (CHN) 54.64
① Time:
② Time:
③ Time:

○ **200 m FREESTYLE**   1992 WINNER N.Haislett (USA)
OLYMPIC RECORD H.Friedrich (GDR) 1:57.65
① Time:
② Time:
③ Time:

○ **400 m FREESTYLE**   1992 WINNER D.Hase (GER)
OLYMPIC RECORD J.Evans (USA) 4:03.85
① Time:
② Time:
③ Time:

○ **800 m FREESTYLE**   1992 WINNER J.Evans (USA)
OLYMPIC RECORD J.Evans (USA) 8:20.20
① Time:
② Time:
③ Time:

○ **100 m BACKSTROKE**   1992 WINNER K.Egerszegi (HUN)
OLYMPIC RECORD K.Egerszegi (HUN) 1:00.68
① Time:
② Time:
③ Time:

○ **200 m BACKSTROKE**   1992 WINNER K.Egerszegi (HUN)
OLYMPIC RECORD K.Egerszegi (HUN) 2:07.06
① Time:
② Time:
③ Time:

○ **100 m BREASTSTROKE '92 WINNER** Y.Roudkovskaia (EUN)
OLYMPIC RECORD T.Dangalakova (BUL) 1:07.95
① Time:
② Time:
③ Time:

DID YOU KNOW ?

● Freestyle means any stroke, but swimmers always use front crawl because it is the fastest.

● A row of flags hangs above the pool 5 m from each end to let backstrokers know when they are close.

● The Olympic swimming pool is 1.8 m deep.

SYNCHRONIZED SWIMMING

This new sport consists of ballet-like movements performed to music (*left*). From 1984 to 1992 the USA and Canada won all the solo and duet gold medals. In 1996, however, there is just one team event instead.

THE AMAZING USA

FREESTYLE VICTORS

In 1992 US women won three individual swimming golds and two team golds. They won both relay events in new Olympic and world record times. Overall, the USA have won more gold medals in women's swimming than any other nation.

Janet Evans (*above*) won the 800 m freestyle in 1988 and again in 1992.

In 1992 the American 4x100 m freestyle team (*above*) won gold and broke the Olympic and world records.

○ **200 m BREASTSTROKE**   1992 WINNER K.Iwasaki (JPN)
   OLYMPIC RECORD K.Iwasaki (JPN) 2:26.65
(1) Time:
(2) Time:
(3) Time:

○ **100 m BUTTERFLY**   1992 WINNER H.Qian (CHN)
   OLYMPIC RECORD H.Qian (CHN) 58.62
(1) Time:
(2) Time:
(3) Time:

○ **200 m BUTTERFLY**   1992 WINNER S.Sanders (USA)
   OLYMPIC RECORD M.Meagher (USA) 2:06.90
(1) Time:
(2) Time:
(3) Time:

○ **200 m INDIV. MEDLEY**   1992 WINNER L.Lin (CHN)
   OLYMPIC RECORD L.Lin (CHN) 2:11.65
(1) Time:
(2) Time:
(3) Time:

○ **400 m INDIV. MEDLEY** 1992 WINNER K.Egerszegi (HUN)
   OLYMPIC RECORD P.Schneider (GDR) 4:36.29
(1) Time:
(2) Time:
(3) Time:

○ **4x100 m FREESTYLE RELAY**   1992 WINNER USA
   OLYMPIC RECORD USA 3:39.46
(1) Time:
(2) Time:
(3) Time:

○ **4x100 m MEDLEY RELAY**   1992 WINNER USA
   OLYMPIC RECORD USA 4:02.54
(1) Time:
(2) Time:
(3) Time:

○ **4x200 m FREESTYLE RELAY**   NEW EVENT
(1) Time:
(2) Time:
(3) Time:

○ **SYNCHRONIZED TEAM**   NEW EVENT
(1)
(2)
(3)

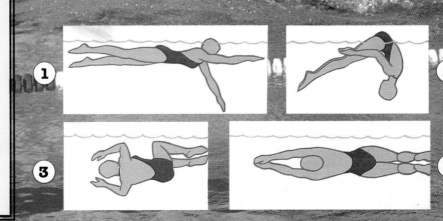

RACING TURN

Front-crawl swimmers (1) use a "tumble" turn, with a front somersault (2) and half twist (3) as they kick off from the wall (4). They can turn without touching the wall with their hands.

DIVING

THE SPORT of diving dates back to the 17th century, when gymnasts in Sweden and Germany practised their spiralling moves by plunging into the sea. Diving branched away from gymnastics just over a hundred years ago, and a men's competition was held at the 1904 Olympics. Women's diving was included eight years later in Stockholm.

There are two separate events: springboard and platform or highboard diving. Both boards are used by men and women. The springboard is three metres above the water and is flexible; its amount of spring can be adjusted by the diver. The rigid platform is 10 metres above the water: about the height of a three-storey building!

In all four events, each diver has to execute a series of preliminary dives, and is then free to attempt more difficult dives. The judges mark a dive out of 10. The highest and lowest marks are ignored, and the rest are added together. This total is then multiplied by a number according to that particular dive's degree of difficulty. So an easy dive performed well can score more points than a difficult dive performed less well. The judges take the whole dive into account: the approach, take-off, technique and grace in the air, and entry into the water.

When the diver enters the water, his or her body should be as near vertical as possible, with head tucked in, feet together and toes pointed. A well-performed dive should make very little splash in the water.

MEN	1992 WINNERS
○ SPRINGBOARD: 11 dives	M.Lenzi (USA)

1   Points:
   2   Points:
     3   Points:

○ PLATFORM: 10 dives	S.Sun (CHN)

1   Points:
   2   Points:
     3   Points:

WOMEN	1992 WINNERS
○ SPRINGBOARD: 10 dives	M.Gao (CHN)

1   Points:
   2   Points:
     3   Points:

○ PLATFORM: 8 dives	F.Mingxia (CHN)

1   Points:
   2   Points:
     3   Points:

LEAPING TO GOLD

Fu Mingxia of China on her way to gold from the women's platform in 1992 (*above*). Two years earlier, Fu had become the youngest world diving champion ever, at the age of 11. The world and Olympic minimum age limit has since been raised to 14.

SPRINGBOARD DIVE

Jorge Mondragon of Mexico (*above*) gracefully enters the water from the springboard in the 1992 Games. Men's springboard proved to be the only diving event in which the Chinese failed to take gold. It was won by Mark Lenzi of the USA, making a third consecutive win for the United States. Will they win it for a fourth time in Atlanta?

TYPES OF DIVE

The five basic types of dive can be performed from either board, and may be embellished. In forward (1) and reverse dives (2), the diver faces the water. In backward (3) and inward dives (4), he or she faces the board. In a twist dive (5), any of the previous four dives is performed with a body twist in the air.

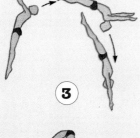

(1)

(2)

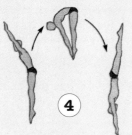

(3)

(4)

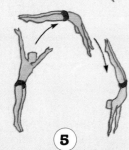

(5)

WATER POLO

INVENTED IN England in 1870, water polo has been an Olympic sport since 1900. Like diving, it is run by the International Swimming Federation. A water polo team is made up of six players and a goalkeeper, and a game consists of four seven-minute quarters. The players try to score goals by passing a ball and throwing it into the opponents' net. Hungary has won the tournament most often, with six golds.

ONE-GOLD DEADLOCK

Since 1900, the USA and Germany (*below*) have won only one gold each, in 1904 and 1928. In 1992, the honour went to Italy for the third time.

○ WATER POLO		1992 WINNER ITA
(1)		
(2)		
(3)		

POLO HATS

Water polo players wear coloured hats with special ear protectors (*left*). The team colours are usually white and blue, and goalkeepers have red hats.

PICK YOUR WINNERS

WHO DO YOU think will win the track and field events in Atlanta? You can fill in your predictions in the table below. To help you make your prediction, the current world champions have been listed. Will they also be winners in the Atlanta Games? You can also find out who won the 1992 Olympic Games in Barcelona by looking at the tables featured on the athletics pages. After each event has taken place, check if your prediction was right by looking back at these tables, where you will have filled in the 1996 gold-, silver- and bronze-medal winners.

	MEN		WOMEN	
	1995 WORLD CHAMPION	**ATLANTA FORECAST**	**1995 WORLD CHAMPION**	**ATLANTA FORECAST**
100 m	Donovan Bailey (CAN)		Gwen Torrence (USA)	
200 m	Michael Johnson (USA)		Merlene Ottey (JAM)	
400 m	Michael Johnson (USA)		Marie-José Pérec (FRA)	
800 m	Wilson Kipketer (DEN)		Ana Quirot (CUB)	
1500 m	Noureddine Morceli (ALG)		Hassiba Boulmerka (ALG)	
5000 m	Ismael Kirui (KEN)		Sonia O'Sullivan (IRL)	
10000 m	Haile Gebrselassie (ETH)		Fernanda Ribeiro (POR)	
100 m hurdles	—	—	Gail Devers (USA)	
110 m hurdles	Allen Johnson (USA)		—	—
400 m hurdles	Derrick Adkins (USA)		Kim Batten (USA)	
3000 m steeplechase	Moses Kiptanui (KEN)		—	—
marathon	Martin Fiz (ESP)		Manuela Machado (POR)	
heptathlon	—	—	Ghada Shouaa (SYR)	
decathlon	Dan O'Brien (USA)		—	—
high jump	Troy Kemp (BAH)		Stefka Kostadinova (BUL)	
long jump	Ivan Pedroso (CUB)		Fiona May (ITA)	
triple jump	Jonathan Edwards (GBR)		Inessa Kravets (UKR)	
pole vault	Sergei Bubka (UKR)		—	—
shot put	John Godina (USA)		Astrid Kumbernuss (GER)	
discus	L. Riedel (GER)		Ellina Svereva (BLR)	
javelin	Jan Zelezny (CZE)		Natalya Shikolenko (BLR)	
hammer	Andrey Abduvaliyev (TJK)		—	—

FASTEST MAN IN THE WORLD?

Donovan Bailey of Canada (*right*, centre) won the 100 m at the Gothenburg world championships in 1995. His fellow Canadian, Bruny Surin (*right*, far right), was second. Ato Boldon of Trinidad (*right*, on the left) took the bronze medal. Will one of them take gold in Atlanta?

NEW WOMEN'S DISTANCE

Ireland's Sonia O'Sullivan (*left*) won the world championship 5000 m in Gothenburg, ahead of Fernanda Ribeiro of Portugal, the 10000-m winner, and Zohra Quaziz of Morocco. Will one of these three runners win the first-ever Olympic 5000 m for women?

CHAMPION TRIPLE JUMPER

Britain's Jonathan Edwards (*above*) broke his own triple-jump world record with his first jump in the 1995 world championships. Then with his second jump he broke the record again, leaping 18.29 m! Olympic champion Mike Conley of the USA was seventh in Gothenburg.

MEDAL TABLES

Which nations will win most gold medals in Atlanta? Make your own forecast for the top 10 nations (*below*). At the end of the Games, fill in the final medals and see how well you did. To help you make your choice, look at the 1896–1992 medal record and the list for the Barcelona Olympics, also on the table below.

GOLD-MEDAL WINNERS			
	1896–1992	BARCELONA 1992	ATLANTA FORECAST	ATLANTA FINAL MEDALS TABLE
1	USA 789	EUN * 45		
2	URS/EUN * 442	USA 37		
3	GER ** 340	GER 33		
4	GBR 177	CHN 16		
5	FRA 161	CUB 14		
6	ITA 153	ESP 13		
7	HUN 136	KOR 12		
8	SWE 133	HUN 11		
9	FIN 98	FRA 8		
10	JPN 90	AUS 7		
	*now RUS and other countries ** including GDR and FRG			

GYMNASTICS

LIKE SO MANY sports, gymnastics was popular in ancient Greece, where it was used as a way of training young men to be fit for battle. The modern form of gymnastics began in the early 1800s in Sweden. By the late 19th century, gymnastics clubs had sprung up in Germany and other European countries. The 1896 Olympics became the first large meeting of gymnasts of modern times. But still only five countries took part, in five different events: pommel horse, rings, horse vault, parallel bars and horizontal bar. The last three events were all won by German gymnasts. At the next Olympics, in Paris, an individual all-round competition was added. Four years later, in St Louis, the first team event was held. The eighth event, floor exercises, was not added until the 1932 Games, in Los Angeles.

The gymnastics competition is in three parts. First, all the gymnasts perform in six events on all the apparatus. Individual scores are added together to decide the result of the team event. The gymnasts with the highest individual scores then go forward to the all-round final. They again compete on all the apparatus, and the totals determine the individual all-round medals. In the third part of the competition, the earlier top scorers go on to the six individual apparatus finals.

CHINESE WIN

Li Xiaosahuang of China (*left*) won the floor exercises in Barcelona. He and his five colleagues also won silver in the team event.

ON THE POMMEL HORSE

The gymnast swings his body around the apparatus continuously, placing one or both hands on the pommels, or handles, as well as on the padded horse. He may swing both legs over the horse together (1) or separately (2), or make scissor movements with his legs (3). Strength, balance and control are essential qualities.

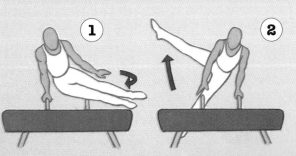

HORIZONTAL GOLD

Trent Dimas of the USA won gold in the horizontal bar event in Barcelona (*above*). This was the only medal won by the USA in the 1992 men's gymnastics.

QUIZ . . . . . .

1 Gymnastics comes from the Greek word gymnos. What does this mean?
   a) strong
   b) clever
   c) naked

2 How large is the area for floor exercises?
   a) 6 sq m
   b) 12 sq m
   c) 18 sq m

3 In gymnastics, what is a flip-flop?
   a) back handspring
   b) gym shoe
   c) poor performance

Answers on page 80

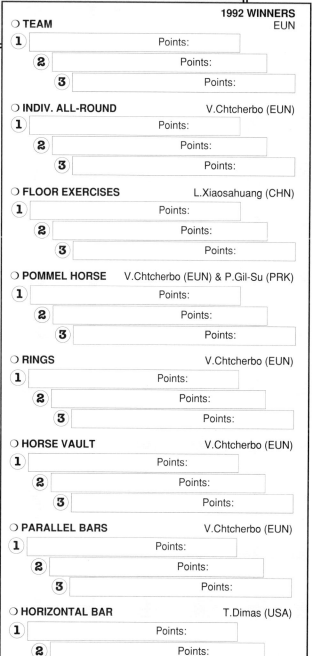

ON THE RINGS

The rings hang 2.75 m above the floor from two wires that are 50 cm apart. They should remain almost stationary and not swing apart as the gymnast performs a series of moves, including legs held straight (1), complete circles (2) and handstands (3).

THE UNIFIED TEAM

At the 1992 Barcelona Olympics, former states of the Soviet Union competed as a Unified Team, representing the newly formed Commonwealth of Independent States. In men's gymnastics, the Unified Team collected six gold medals, including five won by Vitaly Chtcherbo, from Belarus. They won gold, silver and bronze in the all-round competition! But this great Unified Team appeared at only one Olympic Games. In Atlanta, the individual countries, such as Russia and Belarus, will be represented separately.

SIX-MEDAL MAN

Twenty-year-old Vitaly Chtcherbo of the Unified Team won the 1992 Olympic parallel bars (*above*) with a score of 9.9 out of a possible 10.0. He won five other events too!

1992 WINNERS

○ **TEAM**   EUN
1   Points:
2   Points:
3   Points:

○ **INDIV. ALL-ROUND**   V.Chtcherbo (EUN)
1   Points:
2   Points:
3   Points:

○ **FLOOR EXERCISES**   L.Xiaosahuang (CHN)
1   Points:
2   Points:
3   Points:

○ **POMMEL HORSE**   V.Chtcherbo (EUN) & P.Gil-Su (PRK)
1   Points:
2   Points:
3   Points:

○ **RINGS**   V.Chtcherbo (EUN)
1   Points:
2   Points:
3   Points:

○ **HORSE VAULT**   V.Chtcherbo (EUN)
1   Points:
2   Points:
3   Points:

○ **PARALLEL BARS**   V.Chtcherbo (EUN)
1   Points:
2   Points:
3   Points:

○ **HORIZONTAL BAR**   T.Dimas (USA)
1   Points:
2   Points:
3   Points:

GYMNASTICS

Women's events

WOMEN'S GYMNASTICS was introduced as an Olympic competition in 1928. First there is a team event, then an individual all-round competition, and finally individual apparatus finals on the asymmetrical (uneven) bars, balance beam, horse vault and in floor exercises. In addition there is a rhythmic gymnastics competition. The vault event differs from the men's competition; women vault across the width of the horse, while men leap the length of the horse.

Women's gymnastics has increasingly caught the imagination of spectators, as tiny young superstars have taken to the apparatus. In 1972 Olga Korbut of the Soviet Union won the hearts of the audience as she performed superbly to win gold on both the beam and the floor. In 1976 Nadia Comaneci of Romania won three gold medals and became the first gymnast to score a perfect 10.0 in an Olympic competition. But in the record books, no-one can compete with the Soviet gymnast Larissa Latynina. In three Olympic Games ending in 1964 she won 18 medals, including nine gold! This gives her the overall Olympic record for most medals in any sport.

LEAPING FROM THE BARS

Lavinia Milosovici of Romania, performing on the asymmetrical bars (*above*). When they perform on the bars, many gymnasts wear handstraps for protection (*inset*). They also put plenty of white powder on their hands to absorb perspiration and improve grip. The powder is magnesium carbonate, commonly called "chalk". The bars are 350 cm long, and are arranged parallel to each other; one is 140–160 cm above the floor and the other 235–240 cm. The two supporting frames are 43 cm apart.

THE BALANCE BEAM

Acrobatic ability is needed on the wooden beam, which is 5.0 m long and 1.2 m off the floor. Most importantly, it is only 10 cm wide! Suppleness, a fine sense of balance and grace are required, as shown by the split-leg handstand (1) and the splits (2). The gymnast must find a smooth method of getting in and out of each position.

①　②　③

	1992 WINNERS
○ **TEAM**	**EUN**
① _____ Points:	
② _____ Points:	
③ _____ Points:	
○ **INDIVIDUAL ALL-ROUND**	T.Gutsu (EUN)
① _____ Points:	
② _____ Points:	
③ _____ Points:	
○ **HORSE VAULT**	H.Ónodi (HUN) & L.Milosovici (ROM)
① _____ Points:	
② _____ Points:	
③ _____ Points:	
○ **ASYMMETRICAL (UNEVEN) BARS**	L.Lu (CHN)
① _____ Points:	
② _____ Points:	
③ _____ Points:	
○ **BALANCE BEAM**	T.Lysenko (EUN)
① _____ Points:	
② _____ Points:	
③ _____ Points:	
○ **FLOOR EXERCISES**	L.Milosovici (ROM)
① _____ Points:	
② _____ Points:	
③ _____ Points:	
○ **RHYTHMIC INDIV. ALL-ROUND**	A.Timoschenko (EUN)
① _____ Points:	
② _____ Points:	
③ _____ Points:	
○ **RHYTHMIC TEAM ALL-ROUND**	**NEW EVENT**
① _____ Points:	
② _____ Points:	
③ _____ Points:	

THE FORWARD WALKOVER

Poise and control are needed in all the floor exercises. In the forward walkover, the gymnast stretches forward (1), performs a split-leg handstand (2) and brings one leg down while keeping her hands on the floor (3).

KEEPING THE RHYTHM

The rhythmic gymnastics competition was won in Barcelona by Alexandra Timoschenko, age 20, of the Unified Team (*below*). The event was first introduced, as an individual event, at Los Angeles in 1984. In this graceful sport, the gymnasts are accompanied by music as they handle a hoop, ribbon, ball, rope and clubs. In Atlanta, a rhythmic team competition will be held for the first time.

PEOPLE HAVE always tested their strength by lifting heavy weights, and competitions for lifting huge stones were held separately from the ancient Olympic Games. Over two thousand years later, weightlifting is as popular as ever. It was included in the first modern Olympics as a men-only competition, which it has remained.

In 1896 there were just two events, one-arm and two-arm lifts; the bodyweight of the competitors was not significant. But in 1920, five weight classes — determined by body-weight — were introduced. From 1948 the number steadily increased, and there are now 10 in total. These are unofficially called, from the lightest to the heaviest: flyweight, bantam-weight, featherweight, lightweight, middle-weight, 100-kilogram, light-heavyweight, middle-heavyweight, heavyweight and super-heavyweight. Since 1992, the bodyweights for these categories have changed. The lightest lifters now weigh up to 54 kilograms (formerly they weighed up to 52 kilograms), and the heaviest over 108 kilograms (formerly they were over 110 kilograms).

From 1928 to 1972, the winner of each weight class was the competitor who lifted the heaviest combined weight in the three lifts: the press, snatch and clean and jerk. In 1972 the press was dropped. Today, each competitor can attempt three successively heavier lifts in his class, using the snatch and the clean and jerk. He can make three attempts at each weight.

○ **54 kg**	**1992 WINNER (52 kg)** I.Ivanov (BUL)
①	Weight:
②	Weight:
③	Weight:
○ **59 kg**	**1992 WINNER (56 kg)** C.Byung-Kwan (KOR)
①	Weight:
②	Weight:
③	Weight:
○ **64 kg**	**1992 WINNER (60 kg)** N.Suleymanoglü (TUR)
①	Weight:
②	Weight:
③	Weight:
○ **70 kg**	**1992 WINNER (67.5 kg)** I.Militossian (EUN)
①	Weight:
②	Weight:
③	Weight:
○ **76 kg**	**1992 WINNER (75 kg)** F.Kassapu (EUN)
①	Weight:
②	Weight:
③	Weight:

THE SNATCH

The snatch must be made in one single move-ment, with the bar being lifted from the floor to an overhead position. The lifter lifts the weight from the floor (1), goes into a squat position under the bar with arms held straight (2) and then stands up with arms locked (3).

WINNING GOLD

In each weight class, the gold medal is won by the competitor who lifts the greatest total weight. His weights in the two different lifts — the snatch and the clean and jerk — are added together. If two or more competitors tie, the one with the lowest bodyweight is the winner. In 1992, Aleksandr Kourlovitch of Belarus (*right*) — lifting for the Unified Team (EUN) — won his second successive super-heavyweight gold.

○ **83 kg** **1992 WINNER (82.5 kg)** P.Dimas (GRE)

① _____ Weight: ____

② _____ Weight: ____

③ _____ Weight: ____

○ **91 kg** **1992 WINNER (90 kg)** K.Kakhiachvili (EUN)

① _____ Weight: ____

② _____ Weight: ____

③ _____ Weight: ____

○ **99 kg** **1992 WINNER (100 kg)** V.Tregoubov (EUN)

① _____ Weight: ____

② _____ Weight: ____

③ _____ Weight: ____

○ **108 kg** **1992 WINNER (110 kg)** R.Weller (GER)

① _____ Weight: ____

② _____ Weight: ____

③ _____ Weight: ____

○ **over 108 kg** **1992 WINNER (110+ kg)** A.Kourlovitch (EUN)

① _____ Weight: ____

② _____ Weight: ____

③ _____ Weight: ____

DID YOU KNOW ?

● Three referees judge each lift; if they disagree, the majority decision counts.

● Top heavyweights lift about twice their own body weight on average.

THE CLEAN AND JERK

This lift involves two separate actions. In the "clean", the bar is lifted from the ground, with the lifter going up onto his toes (1). With the bar on his shoulders (2), he then — in the "jerk" — thrusts the bar to an overhead position (3).

① ② ③

ANCIENT AND MODERN

THE FIRST recorded Games were held in 776 BC at Olympia, a sacred site in ancient Greece dedicated to the god Zeus. The ancient Greeks held regular festivals here in his honour. These included a sprint race in the stadium on a track 192 metres long. The athletes carried shields and wore helmets, but no clothes!

From 776 BC onwards, the Games took place at four-yearly intervals, called Olympiads; the Games were so important that the Olympiad was used as a way of measuring time. More running events were added, together with jumping, throwing, wrestling and chariot racing. Processions, feasts and poetry recitals remained part of the festival, which came to last for five days. It was forbidden for women and slaves even to watch the Games, let alone take part.

After Rome conquered Greece, the Olympics became less important. Finally, they were banned in AD 393.

Some 1500 years later, a French Baron, Pierre de Coubertin (1863–1937), had the idea of bringing the Olympic Games back (*left*). He convinced sporting authorities all over the world that the revived Games would strengthen young people's bodies and minds, as well as helping international understanding. It was decided to hold the Olympic Games every four years, as before. The first Games of modern times (*below*) were held in the Greek capital, Athens, in 1896. The 1996 Atlanta Games celebrate the 100th anniversary of the first modern Olympics. A phrase often attributed to Baron de Coubertin was: "The most important thing in the Olympic Games is not to win, but to take part".

ANCIENT OLYMPIA

Archaeologists have uncovered the ruins of the site of the original Olympic Games (*below*). There were temples to Zeus, king of the gods, and Hera, Zeus's wife. The stadium, entered through this archway, held over 20,000 spectators, and the athletes trained in a luxurious gymnasium that had hot and cold baths.

100 YEARS

Olympic Venues

1896	Athens, Greece
1900	Paris, France
1904	St Louis, USA
1906	Athens, Greece (extra Games)
1908	London, England
1912	Stockholm, Sweden
1920	Antwerp, Belgium
1924	Paris, France
1928	Amsterdam, Netherlands
1932	Los Angeles, USA
1936	Berlin, Germany
1948	London, England
1952	Helsinki, Finland
1956	Melbourne, Australia
1960	Rome, Italy
1964	Tokyo, Japan
1968	Mexico City, Mexico
1972	Munich, Germany
1976	Montreal, Canada
1980	Moscow, Russia
1984	Los Angeles, USA
1988	Seoul, South Korea
1992	Barcelona, Spain
1996	Atlanta, USA

US ESPEREM A ...
OS ESPERAMOS EN ...
RENDEZ-VOUS À ...
SEE YOU IN ...
ATLANTA 1996

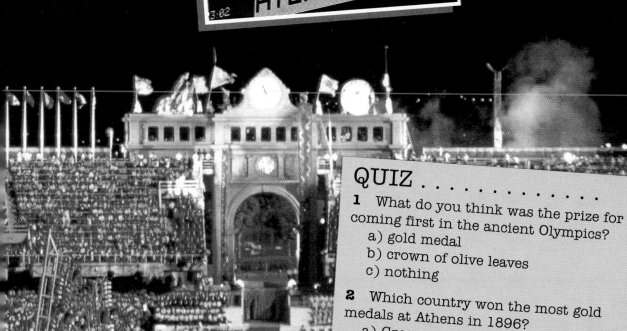

QUIZ . . . .

1 What do you think was the prize for coming first in the ancient Olympics?

    a) gold medal

    b) crown of olive leaves

    c) nothing

2 Which country won the most gold medals at Athens in 1896?

    a) Greece

    b) Germany

    c) USA

3 Where will the Olympic Games be held in 2000?

    a) Sydney

    b) Beijing

    c) Berlin

Answers on page 80

REAL, OR ROYAL, tennis was the favourite sport of French and English kings in the 16th century. The modern game of tennis, which has different rules, was not introduced until the 1870s, when it was played on grass. Today it is also played on hardcourt surfaces. The sport was included in the first eight modern Olympic Games. It was dropped in 1928, and not brought back as a medal competition until 1988, though it was played as a demonstration sport in 1968 and 1984. In 1984, the singles winners were Stefan Edberg of Sweden and Steffi Graf of Germany, both later champions of Wimbledon and many other grand slam tournaments.

There are four Olympic events: singles and doubles for men and women. The singles competitions each contain 64 players, with no more than three allowed to qualify from any one country. There are 32 pairs in the doubles, with only one pair per country allowed to qualify. All matches are played to the best of three sets, except for the men's finals, which are the best of five sets. In Atlanta, bronze medal play-off matches will be held between the losing semi-finalists for the first time. Previously they were awarded to both players or pairs.

THE COURT

Tennis court surfaces are varied; they include grass, wood, concrete, clay and artificial grass. The last Olympic competition was played on clay. Atlanta's tennis centre has a hardcourt surface called "Plexipave". But all courts are the same size, and the net is always 91 cm high in the centre (*right*).

baseline

singles sideline

net 91 cm high at centre

doubles sideline

service line

BATTLING FOR BRONZE

The Australian duo Nicole Provis and Rachael McQuillan (*above*) striking back to take bronze in the women's doubles final in 1992. Gold went to Gigi and Mary Joe Fernandez of the USA.

MEN	1992 WINNERS
○ SINGLES	M.Rosset (SUI)
①	
②	
③	
○ DOUBLES	B.Becker & M.Stich (GER)
①	
②	
③	
WOMEN	
○ SINGLES	J.Capriati (USA)
①	
②	
③	
○ DOUBLES	G.Fernandez & M.J.Fernandez (USA)
①	
②	
③	

TABLE TENNIS

GAMES CALLED "indoor tennis" and "ping pong" were all played in the late 19th century. But table tennis only became an Olympic event in 1988. The bat, or racket, is made of wood covered by a pimpled rubber mat; and the ball is made of celluloid and weighs only 2.5 grams. Five of the eight golds awarded so far have been won by China.

FAST AND FURIOUS

Table tennis is a very fast game, and the Barcelona arena (*below*) was a frenzy of activity. Points are scored by winning rallies, and a game is won by the first player to reach 21 points.

GET A GRIP

Deng Yaping of China, at 19 years old and just 1.55 m tall, won the women's singles in Barcelona (*above*). Many Chinese players use a "pen-hold" grip, but she holds her bat in the "shake-hands" way.

DID YOU KNOW?

● Britain has won more Olympic tennis medals than any other country (but none since 1924!).

● The height of a table tennis net is a fraction less than the height of four table tennis balls on top of one another.

● There will be seeds in the Atlanta tennis competitions, selected by the official referee.

MEN	1992 WINNERS
○ SINGLES	J-O.Waldner (SWE)
①	
②	
③	
○ DOUBLES	L.Lin & T.Wang (CHN)
①	
②	
③	
WOMEN	
○ SINGLES	D.Yaping (CHN)
①	
②	
③	
○ DOUBLES	Q.Hong & D.Yaping (CHN)
①	
②	
③	

BADMINTON

A GAME SIMILAR to badminton was played in China more than two thousand years ago. In India in the 19th century, another version was played, called "poona". This was brought to England by British army officers in about 1870; the new game was named "badminton" after the Duke of Beaufort's residence, Badminton House, where it was probably played indoors for the first time.

Badminton was played at the 1972 Games as a demonstration sport, as an exhibition at Seoul in 1988, and as a medal sport at Barcelona in 1992. There, both singles events were won by Indonesians: the first gold medals ever won by that country. Both doubles events were won by South Koreans, and Malaysia gained its first ever medal by winning the joint bronze, with China, in the men's doubles.

In Atlanta, a mixed doubles competition is included for the first time. At the world grand prix finals in 1994, the mixed doubles was won by Thomas Lund and Marlene Thomson of Denmark, so perhaps a European mixed pair will be able to break Asian domination in Atlanta? At the same tournament, Indonesians won both the singles and the men's doubles events!

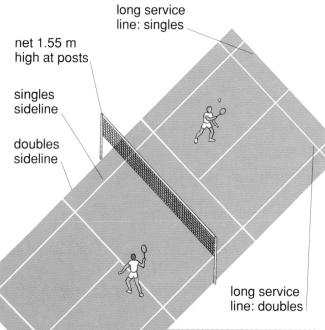

long service line: singles

net 1.55 m high at posts

singles sideline

doubles sideline

long service line: doubles

THE COURT

On court (*above*), the net is 1.55 m high at the posts. As in tennis, there are singles sidelines (or tramlines) and wider doubles sidelines. At the back of the court are serving tramlines: the inner line applies to doubles and the outer line to singles. The outer back line applies to both singles and doubles in general play. A shuttlecock landing on a line is counted as "in".

RACKET AND SHUTTLE

A modern badminton racket is light, flexible and strong (*right*), allowing powerful wrist-action shots. The frame and shaft are moulded from materials such as graphite, carbon and fibreglass. The shuttlecock, or "shuttle" for short (*far right*), is made of goose feathers fixed into a cork base. A small metal weight inside the cork helps the shuttlecock to fly well.

MEN	1992 WINNERS
○ SINGLES	A.B.Kusuma (INA)
①	
②	
③	
○ DOUBLES	M-S.Kim & J-B.Park (KOR)
①	
②	
③	
WOMEN	
○ SINGLES	S.Susanti (INA)
①	
②	
③	
○ DOUBLES	H-Y.Hwang & Y-S.Chung (KOR)
①	
②	
③	
○ MIXED DOUBLES	NEW EVENT
①	
②	
③	

INDONESIAN RIVALRY

Allan Budi Kusuma of Indonesia beat his fellow-countryman, Ardy Wiranata, in the men's singles final at the last Olympics (*left*). In the world grand prix finals of 1994, the two positions were reversed. Will anyone be able to split them up in Atlanta?

SOUTH KOREAN SUCCESS

In the 1992 women's doubles final, the South Korean pair of Hye-Young Hwang and Young-So Chung (*below*, near end) beat their Chinese opponents to win gold. South Korean and Chinese pairs shared the bronze medals as well.

QUIZ . . . .

1 How many points must a badminton player reach to win a game in women's singles?
  a) 11
  b) 15
  c) 21

2 What is the fastest that a shuttlecock can zoom off a racket?
  a) 100 kph
  b) 200 kph
  c) 300 kph

3 How many badminton gold medals will be given out in Atlanta?
  a) 5
  b) 8
  c) 16

Answers on page 80

SERVING POINT

Susi Susanti of Indonesia (*above*), serving her way to gold in 1992. The serve is very important in badminton, especially since only the server scores points. If the receiver wins a rally, she gets the serve and the right to score points.

55

SIXTEEN TEAMS compete for the gold medal in the men's soccer tournament. The USA, as hosts, and defending Olympic champions, Spain, qualify automatically. The other teams come through qualifying rounds. All players must be under 23 years old and can be either amateur or professional, but must not have played in any of the World Cup matches.

Women's soccer scores a first at the Atlanta Games: eight women's teams are playing in an Olympic soccer tournament for the first time. The USA, who won the first women's World Championships in 1991, are hoping to repeat their winning performance and take the gold.

○ MEN	1992 WINNER ESP
1	
2	
3	

○ WOMEN	NEW EVENT
1	
2	
3	

DID YOU KNOW ?

● The word "soccer" comes from as**soc**iation football, with **-cer** added.

● Soccer was the first team sport to be played in the Olympic Games.

● Great Britain and Hungary have won the most gold medals – three each.

● The biggest ever Olympic win was 17–1 by Denmark over France 'A' in 1908.

HOME WINNERS

In the 1992 Olympic final, the host nation, Spain, won 3–2 over Poland in front of 95,000 ecstatic spectators (*left*). The goal on the soccer pitch (*below*) measures 7.32 m wide and 2.44 m high.

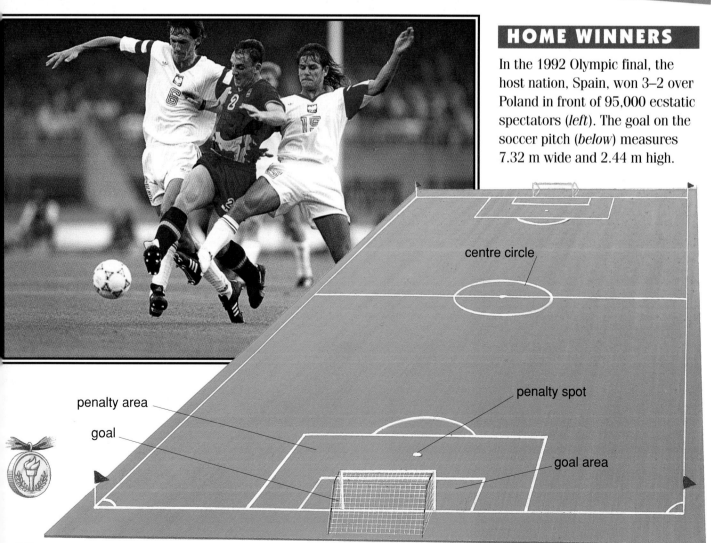

centre circle

penalty spot

penalty area

goal

goal area

HOCKEY

LIKE SOCCER, field hockey is a fast, skilful game played by two teams of 11 players. It is played on artificial grass, so that the ball can run smoothly. In Atlanta there are 12 men's and eight women's teams, both including the Barcelona gold medallists, the current World Cup holders and the US hosts. The other teams had to pre-qualify. While the men play preliminary matches in groups, the women play a round-robin event first, in which all the teams play each other. The top team will then play the second for the gold and silver medals, and the third and fourth teams will play for the bronze.

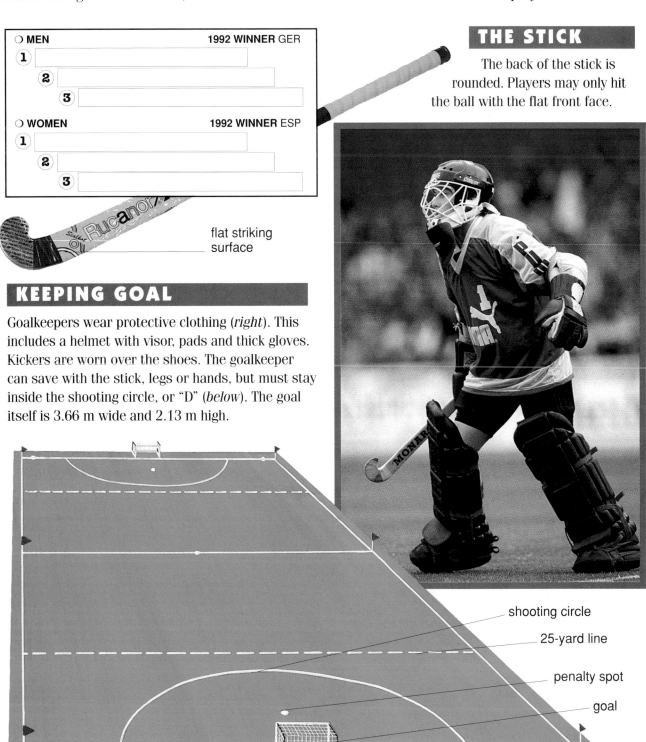

○ MEN		1992 WINNER GER
①		
②		
③		

○ WOMEN		1992 WINNER ESP
①		
②		
③		

THE STICK

The back of the stick is rounded. Players may only hit the ball with the flat front face.

flat striking surface

KEEPING GOAL

Goalkeepers wear protective clothing (*right*). This includes a helmet with visor, pads and thick gloves. Kickers are worn over the shoes. The goalkeeper can save with the stick, legs or hands, but must stay inside the shooting circle, or "D" (*below*). The goal itself is 3.66 m wide and 2.13 m high.

shooting circle

25-yard line

penalty spot

goal

BASKETBALL

THE GAME of basketball was first played in the Olympics at the 1936 Berlin Games. On that occasion the competition was staged outdoors, but ever since it has been held on indoor courts. At the Berlin Games the gold medals were presented to the American team by the modern game's inventor, Dr. James Naismith. In 1891 he had nailed two peach baskets at opposite ends of a balcony at a college in Massachusetts, USA. He then gave two teams of students a soccer ball, which had to be "dropped" into the baskets to score. The roots of the game may date back as early as the 10th century BC to a game called Pok-ta-Pok, played in Mexico by the Olmecs.

Since that first Olympic tournament in 1936, the USA have continued to dominate the men's game. They had an Olympic winning streak of 63 victories that brought them seven gold medals in a row. Overall, the USA have won 10 of the 13 Olympic titles, the other gold medallists being the former Soviet Union and the former Yugoslavia.

Women's basketball was introduced in 1976, and has always been dominated by the USA and the former Soviet Union. They have both won two golds each, with another going to the Unified Team in 1992.

HOT RIVALS

The women's competition in Barcelona was won by the Unified Team, who beat China in the final.

free throw line

centre line

three-points semi-circle

restricted area

basket

ON COURT

The basketball court (*left*) is 28 m long and 15 m wide. At each end is a restricted area. During free throws players must stand at spaces marked along the restricted area. Outside this is a semi-circle. Baskets scored from outside this semi-circle count three points. The centre circle is used to start the game, with a jump-ball. The referee throws the ball into the air between two opposing players, while all non-jumpers stand outside the circle.

THE BASKET

The basket (*right*) is attached to a backboard, at a point 3.05 m above the floor. The ring that supports the cord net is 45 cm wide. The basket is the players' goal, and baskets score points accordingly — one point for a free throw after a rule infringement, two points for an open-play basket, and three points for a basket scored from outside the three-point semi-circle. If the scores are level at the end of normal time, as many five minute periods of overtime as are necessary are played until a player scores.

THE DUNK

A dunk is a basket scored by a player jumping high with the ball and thrusting it down through the net (*below*). It sounds easy, but remember that the basket is over 3 m off the ground.

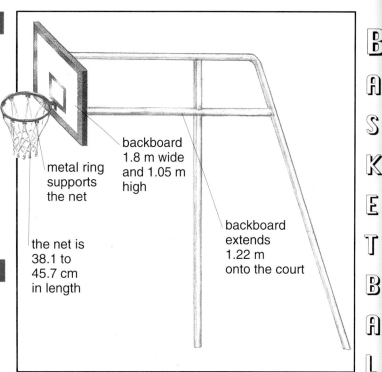

metal ring supports the net

the net is 38.1 to 45.7 cm in length

backboard 1.8 m wide and 1.05 m high

backboard extends 1.22 m onto the court

○ MEN		1992 WINNER USA
1		
2		
3		

○ WOMEN		1992 WINNER EUN
1		
2		
3		

THE "DREAM TEAM"

Before 1992, the USA had always sent a selection of college players to the Olympics. But in Barcelona, they were represented by the best players from the strongest league in the world. The "dream team" (*right*) contained Michael "Air" Jordan, Earvin "Magic" Johnson and other top stars. They beat Croatia in the final to win their expected gold medals.

BASEBALL

BASEBALL is known as the "great American pastime". It was played as a demonstration sport at seven different Olympics, including those of 1984 and 1988, before it was finally accepted as a medal sport at Barcelona in 1992. Japan won the demonstration title in Los Angeles, and the USA in Seoul, but neither of these great baseballing countries could beat Cuba in Barcelona. In Atlanta, eight men's teams will compete for the gold medal.

The aim of the game is to score more runs than the opposing team. One team bats while the other fields. The fielding team pitches to the batter and tries either to catch any ball that is hit, or to touch the batter while he is running between bases; if they succeed, the batter is out. A run is scored when the batter reaches the "home plate".

THE BATTER

The ball must be pitched over the "home plate", a five-sided rubber slab, and must travel below the batter's armpits and above his knees. Here, Shinichi Sato of Japan (*right*) hits a ball that has been correctly pitched. If the batter misses, it is called a strike. After three strikes he is out.

○ BASEBALL	1992 WINNERS CUB
1	
2	
3	

BASEBALL IN ATLANTA

In 1996, Olympic baseball will be played in the Atlanta-Fulton Stadium, home of the famous Atlanta Braves. The Braves' pitcher, Tom Glavine (*left*), helped the Braves win the World Series in 1995. The US Olympic team, made up of top college players, came fourth in Barcelona, and will be hoping to strike gold this time.

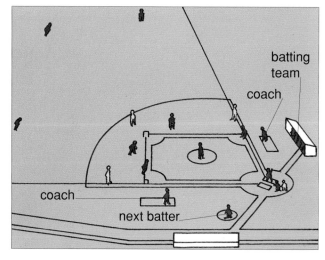

FIELDING POSITIONS IN BASEBALL

The nine fielding positions (*above*, in red) are: a pitcher; a catcher, who stands behind the opposing team's batter; three basemen, on first, second and third bases; a shortstop between the bases; and three fielders in the outfield. The umpires are shown here in yellow, and the batting team in blue.

SOFTBALL

SOFTBALL is a similar game to baseball, and will be played as an Olympic sport for the first time in Atlanta. Eight women's teams will compete for the medals.

The game originated in the USA in 1895 as an indoor form of baseball, and "softball" became its official title in 1933. This name is misleading, because a softball is not soft at all; it is as hard as a baseball! The softball is bigger, heavier and easier to handle, however. The other main differences from baseball are that softball is played on a smaller pitch, the bat is shorter and lighter, and the ball is pitched underarm.

FAST AND FURIOUS

Women's softball is a fast, exciting sport (*right*), and the games in Atlanta are sure to be popular with the watching public. It is said that softball is the most popular team sport in the United States in terms of numbers of players.

PITCHING THE SOFTBALL

The pitcher must stand with both feet on the pitcher's plate, in the middle of the playing diamond, facing the batter (1). The ball must be delivered underarm, with the hand lower than the hips (2). The pitcher may take one step forward towards the batter during the delivery (3). She aims at a strike zone similar to that in baseball — at a level between the batter's armpits and her knees.

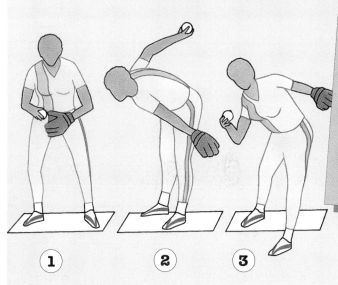

(1) (2) (3)

QUIZ . . . . . .

1 What is the circumference of a baseball?
a) 23 cm
b) 33 cm
c) 43 cm

2 How long is a softball bat?
a) 66 cm
b) 86 cm
c) 106 cm

3 To which city do baseball's Blue Jays belong?
a) Atlanta
b) Boston
c) Toronto

Answers on page 80

○ SOFTBALL   NEW EVENT
(1)
(2)
(3)

VOLLEYBALL

VOLLEYBALL — first played at the Olympics in 1964 — is one of the most p o p u l a r games in the world. Indoor volleyball is played by two teams of six players. The aim is to hit the ball over the net and make it land on the other team's side, or force them to play it out of court or into the net; both of these win points. Each team may touch the ball up to three times before sending it over the net. Points are scored by the serving team, while the receivers can earn the right to serve. Each match is the best of five sets, and a set is won when a team reaches 15 points.

In Atlanta men and women will also play beach volleyball for the first time at a Games. This rapidly growing sport is played by teams of two players on sand. Twenty-four pairs will play in the men's competition, and 16 pairs in the women's.

net and centre line

attack or "spiking" line

serving area

INDOOR COURT

The volleyball court (*above*) has a high net that is 2.43 m above the floor for men, and 2.24 m for women. Play for points begins with three players near the net and three at the back of the court. After the ball is served, players may move anywhere on their side of the net.

SETTING UP

The receiving team generally uses its three touches like this: one player passes the ball, a second — standing between the attack line and the net — sets it up, and a third, also in front of the line, smashes, or "spikes", it over the net (*left*).

MEN		1992 WINNERS
○ VOLLEYBALL		BRA
①		
②		
③		
○ BEACH VOLLEYBALL		NEW EVENT
①		
②		
③		
WOMEN		
○ VOLLEYBALL		CUB
①		
②		
③		
○ BEACH VOLLEYBALL		NEW EVENT
①		
②		
③		

ON THE BEACH

The fast-growing game of beach volleyball (*right*) will surely appeal to the many who will see it for the first time at the Atlanta Games.

HANDBALL

HANDBALL WAS first played in Germany in about 1895. It was introduced to the Olympics in Berlin in 1936 as an 11-a-side outdoor game, and Germany beat Austria in the final. The sport was then left out of the Olympics until 1972, when it was reintroduced in Munich as a seven-a-side indoor game. It has remained this way ever since, and women's handball was added in 1976.

HANDBALL COURT

A goal is scored by throwing the ball past the keeper into the net (*below*). Shots at goal must be taken from outside the goal area. Free throws, which are like free kicks in soccer, are taken outside the outer circle.

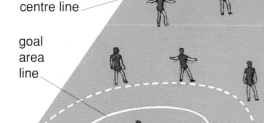

centre line

goal area line

free throw line

SOUTH KOREAN SUCCESS

Oh Sung-Ok of South Korea (*above*) springs into action in the women's final against Norway, helping her country to victory. In 1992 South Korea retained the women's title they won four years earlier in Seoul.

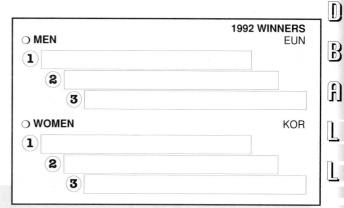

1992 WINNERS		
○ MEN		EUN
①		
②		
③		
○ WOMEN		KOR
①		
②		
③		

MOVING WITH THE BALL

A player with the ball (1) may take three steps before he or she must bounce or pass it (2). If the ball is caught in two hands, the player must shoot or pass within three seconds.

① ②

N THE ancient Olympics of 688 BC, Greek fighters are known to have wrapped their fists in leather straps. The combatants fought until one of them dropped or conceded by raising a fist in the air. The name "boxing" was introduced in England in the 17th century, when men boxed each other with bare fists. Then in 1865 the Marquis of Queensberry drew up new rules that included wearing gloves, and these rules are more or less still in use today.

Boxing came into the modern Olympics in 1904. It is a men-only competition. Gold medals have been won by many boxers who have gone on to become professional champions. World heavyweight champions who, earlier in their careers, won Olympic gold for the USA include such famous names as Floyd Patterson, Cassius Clay (Muhammad Ali), Joe Frazier, George Foreman, Leon Spinks and Ray Mercer. Foreman won the Olympic heavyweight event in 1968, at the age of 20. Twenty-six years later, he was still winning professional title fights!

Olympic boxers must wear headguards, and rules are very strictly enforced. Nevertheless, many people feel that boxing is dangerous and would like it banished as an Olympic sport. Olympic boxing is under the microscope.

USA BOX ON

Lightweight Oscar de la Hoye (*below*) won the USA's only boxing gold medal in Barcelona, when he beat Marco Rudolph of Germany. Since 1904, the USA have won 47 Olympic golds for boxing, and American boxers are keen to add to this number on their home territory of Atlanta.

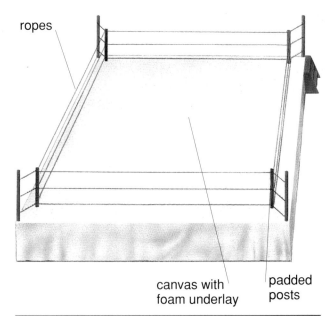

ropes

canvas with foam underlay

padded posts

RING AND REFEREE

When is a ring square? When it's a boxing ring! A bout is scored by a panel of judges, and controlled in the ring by the referee.

1992 WINNERS

○ **LIGHT-FLYWEIGHT: under 48 kg**   R.Marcelo (CUB)
1.
2.
3.

○ **FLYWEIGHT: 51 kg**   C.Choi (PRK)
1.
2.
3.

○ **BANTAMWEIGHT: 54 kg**   J.Casamayor (CUB)
1.
2.
3.

○ **FEATHERWEIGHT: 57 kg**   A.Tews (GER)
1.
2.
3.

○ **LIGHTWEIGHT: 60 kg**   O.de la Hoye (USA)
1.
2.
3.

○ **LIGHT-WELTERWEIGHT: 63.5 kg**   H.Vincent (CUB)
1.
2.
3.

FOULS

The referee usually cautions a boxer who commits a foul. Fouls include: hitting "below the belt" (1), a "rabbit punch" on the back of the head or neck (2), punching in the kidneys (3), head butting (4), punching with the non-knuckle area of the glove (5) and holding (6).

1992 WINNERS

○ WELTERWEIGHT: 67 kg — M.Carruth (IRL)
1
2
3

○ LIGHT-MIDDLEWEIGHT: 71 kg — J.Lemus (CUB)
1
2
3

○ MIDDLEWEIGHT: 75 kg — A.Hernández (CUB)
1
2
3

○ LIGHT-HEAVYWEIGHT: 81 kg — T.May (GER)
1
2
3

○ HEAVYWEIGHT: 91 kg — F.Savon (CUB)
1
2
3

○ SUPER-HEAVYWEIGHT: over 91 kg — R.Balado (CUB)
1
2
3

THE GREATEST EVER?

Cassius Clay (later Muhammad Ali) of the USA (*below*, left) won the light-heavyweight gold at the 1960 Olympics. In 1964 he became professional world heavyweight champion. Here he lands a punch on Cleveland Williams of the USA in 1966. In 1974 Ali regained the title (having been stripped of it in 1967) by defeating George Foreman. In 1978 he won it for a third time from Leon Spinks.

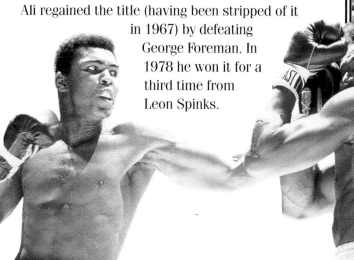

SEVEN CUBAN GOLDS

Roberto Balado of Cuba (*above*, right) beating Richard Igbinegha of Nigeria in the super-heavyweight division of the 1992 Olympics. Cuba won an amazing seven gold medals out of 12 in Barcelona. This brought the country's total to 19 boxing golds in the history of the Games.

WRESTLING

WRESTLERS are known to have fought in the ancient Olympics of 708 BC, and the sport was included in the 1896 Games as a men-only event, which it has remained. In the 1896 Games, Greco-Roman wrestling was the only category, and there was no bodyweight limit. Freestyle was introduced in 1904. The main difference between the categories is that in Greco-Roman the use of legs and holds below the waist are not allowed. Today there are 10 bodyweight classes in both categories, ranging from light-flyweight (under 48 kilograms) to super-heavyweight (over 100 kilograms).

A wrestler may win a match if he succeeds in pinning his opponent's shoulder blades to the mat for half a second. But most wrestling matches are won on points, awarded for performing special moves.

GRECO-ROMAN LIGHT-HEAVYWEIGHT CHAMPION

Maik Bullmann of Germany (*above*) was Greco-Roman light-heavyweight world champion from 1989 to 1991. He then won gold in Barcelona in 1992 by beating Hakki Basar of Turkey in the final.

BARCELONA FREESTYLE FINALISTS

Hak-Son Li of North Korea won flyweight gold in 1992 by beating J.R. Jones of the USA (*above,* Li on top). The use of legs, prohibited in Greco-Roman wrestling, is clearly visible here.

GRECO-ROMAN	1992 WINNERS
○ LIGHT-FLYWEIGHT: 48 kg	O.Koutcherenko (EUN)
①	
○ FLYWEIGHT: 52 kg	J.Rønningen (NOR)
①	
○ BANTAMWEIGHT: 57 kg	A.Han-Bong (KOR)
①	
○ FEATHERWEIGHT: 62 kg	M.Pirim (TUR)
①	
○ LIGHTWEIGHT: 68 kg	A.Repka (HUN)
①	
○ WELTERWEIGHT: 74 kg	M.Iskandarian (EUN)
①	
○ MIDDLEWEIGHT: 82 kg	P.Farkas (HUN)
①	
○ LIGHT-HEAVYWEIGHT: 90 kg	M.Bullmann (GER)
①	
○ HEAVYWEIGHT: 100 kg	H.Milian (CUB)
①	
○ SUPER-HEAVYWEIGHT: over 100 kg	A.Kareline (EUN)
①	

FREESTYLE	1992 WINNERS
○ LIGHT-FLYWEIGHT: 48 kg	I.Kim (PRK)
①	
○ FLYWEIGHT: 52 kg	H-S.Li (PRK)
①	
○ BANTAMWEIGHT: 57 kg	A.Diaz (CUB)
①	
○ FEATHERWEIGHT: 62 kg	J.Smith (USA)
①	
○ LIGHTWEIGHT: 68 kg	A.Fadzaev (EUN)
①	
○ WELTERWEIGHT: 74 kg	J-S.Park (KOR)
①	
○ MIDDLEWEIGHT: 82 kg	K.Jackson (USA)
①	
○ LIGHT-HEAVYWEIGHT: 90 kg	M.Khadartsev (EUN)
①	
○ HEAVYWEIGHT: 100 kg	L.Khabelov (EUN)
①	
○ SUPER-HEAVYWEIGHT: over 100 kg	B.Baumgartner (USA)
①	

JUDO

JUDO FIRST became an Olympic sport in Tokyo, in 1964. Meaning "the gentle way", it developed from the martial art of jujitsu, which teaches self-defence and a whole way of behaving. The women's Olympic judo competition was introduced as recently as 1992.

There are five groups of throwing techniques: hand, hip, back, side and foot or leg throws. Each group contains three types of throw. A judoka, or judo contestant, wins a match by throwing the opponent on his or her back, or by holding the opponent there for 30 seconds. A win can also be achieved by forcing a submission or from a decision by the judges.

HOME WIN IN SPAIN

Miriam Blasco of Spain beat Britain's Nicola Fairbrother in the final of the under 56 kg division in Barcelona (*left*). The Spaniard won gold in front of 6,000 home spectators. Fairbrother went on to win the 1993 world championship in Canada.

UCHI MATA

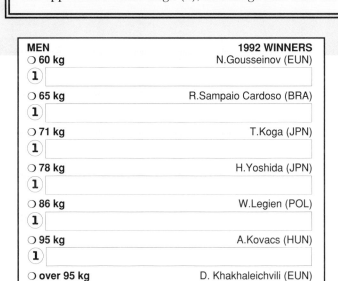

Uchi mata, or the inner thigh throw, is one of the three foot- or leg-throwing techniques. The thrower (the left contestant here) grasps his opponent (1), twists round with his leg against the opponent's inner thigh (2), and flings him onto his back (3).

MEN	1992 WINNERS
○ **60 kg**	N.Gousseinov (EUN)
①	
○ **65 kg**	R.Sampaio Cardoso (BRA)
①	
○ **71 kg**	T.Koga (JPN)
①	
○ **78 kg**	H.Yoshida (JPN)
①	
○ **86 kg**	W.Legien (POL)
①	
○ **95 kg**	A.Kovacs (HUN)
①	
○ **over 95 kg**	D. Khakhaleichvili (EUN)
①	

WOMEN	1992 WINNERS
○ **48 kg**	C.Nowak (FRA)
①	
○ **52 kg**	A.Munoz Martinez (ESP)
①	
○ **56 kg**	M.Blasco (ESP)
①	
○ **61 kg**	C.Fleury (FRA)
①	
○ **66 kg**	O.Reve Jimenez (CUB)
①	
○ **72 kg**	M-J.Kim (KOR)
①	
○ **over 72 kg**	X.Zhuang (CHN)
①	

CANOEING

THERE ARE two types of canoe: kayaks and Canadian canoes. In kayaks, competitors use paddles with a blade at each end; in Canadian canoes they use a paddle with a single blade, and half-kneel rather than sit. In the race names, K stands for kayak, C for Canadian canoe, and the number indicates how many canoeists are in the boat. So K-2 is a race for kayak pairs. In slalom events the canoeists race down wild water, steering between gate poles.

WOMEN'S KAYAK

Women race only in kayaks. In the last Olympics, the K-4 race (*above*) was the only one of the four women's events in which Germany did not take gold.

WOMEN	1992 WINNERS
○ K-1 500 m	B.Schmidt (GER)
①	Time:
○ K-2 500 m	R.Portwich & A.Von Seck (GER)
①	Time:
○ K-4 500 m	HUN
①	Time:
○ K-1 slalom	E.Micheler (GER)
①	Time:

MEN	1992 WINNERS
○ K-1 500 m	M.Kolehmainen (FIN)
①	Time:
○ K-1 1000 m	C.Robinson (AUS)
①	Time:
○ K-2 500 m	K.Bluhm & T.Gütsche (GER)
①	Time:
○ K-2 1000 m	K.Bluhm & T.Gütsche (GER)
①	Time:
○ K-4 1000 m	GER
①	Time:
○ C-1 500 m	N.Boukhalov (BUL)
①	Time:
○ C-1 1000 m	N.Boukhalov (BUL)
①	Time:
○ C-2 500 m	A.Masseikov & D.Dovgalenok (EUN)
①	Time:
○ C-2 1000 m	U.Papke & I.Spelly (GER)
①	Time:
○ K-1 slalom	P.Ferrazzi (ITA)
①	Time:
○ C-1 slalom	L.Pollert (TCH)
①	Time:
○ C-2 slalom	S.Strausbaugh & J.Jacobi (USA)
①	Time:

ROWING

ROWING BEGAN as an Olympic sport for men in 1900, and for women in 1976. All events take place over a straight, 2000-metre course, and begin with qualifying races. In 1996 there are three new events: men's and women's lightweight double sculls and men's lightweight coxless (i.e. no extra person steering) fours.

FOUR IN A ROW?

At Barcelona in 1992, the coxless pairs race was won by the British duo Matthew Pinsent and Steve Redgrave (*right*, Redgrave on the right). Redgrave had already won gold in the two previous Olympics: in the coxed fours in 1984 and coxless pairs in 1988. If he can win a fourth consecutive gold in Atlanta, he will be the first rower ever to do so.

YACHTING

YACHTING HAS been an Olympic sport since 1896, though in that year all races were cancelled due to bad weather! There are seven boat classes in 1996. The 470 is a centreboard dinghy, 4.70 metres long. Finn and Europe are smaller single-handed boats. Star and Soling are two- and three-person keel-boats. Tornado is a two-person catamaran (a twin-hulled boat), and Laser — a new event in 1996 — is a flat-topped, single-handed boat (the sailor sits on, rather than in, the boat). There is also a boardsailing (or windsurfing) class called Mistral.

MEN	1992 WINNERS
○ 470	J.Calafat & F.Sánchez (ESP)
①	
○ FINN	J.van der Ploeg Garcia (ESP)
①	
○ MISTRAL (BOARDSAILING)	F.David (FRA)
①	
WOMEN	
○ 470	T.Zabell & P.Guerra (ESP)
①	
○ EUROPE	L.Andersen (NOR)
①	
○ MISTRAL (BOARDSAILING)	B-A.Kendall (NZL)
①	
MIXED	
○ SOLING	DEN
①	
○ STAR	M.Reynolds & H.Haenel (USA)
①	
○ LASER	NEW EVENT
①	
○ TORNADO	Y.Loday & N.Hénard (FRA)
①	

SAILING IN A SOLING

In 1992, the Danish crew of Jesper Bank, Steen Secher and Jesper Seier (*above*) won in the largest Olympic class, the three-handed Soling competition.

ROWING MEN	1992 WINNERS
○ SINGLE SCULLS	T.Lange (GER)
①	Time:
○ DOUBLE SCULLS	P.Antonie & M.Hawkins (AUS)
①	Time:
○ QUADRUPLE SCULLS	GER
①	Time:
○ COXLESS PAIRS	M.Pinsent & S.Redgrave (GBR)
①	Time:
○ COXLESS FOURS	AUS
①	Time:
○ EIGHTS	CAN
①	Time:
○ LIGHTWEIGHT DOUBLE SCULLS	NEW EVENT
①	Time:
○ LIGHTWEIGHT COXLESS FOURS	NEW EVENT
①	Time:
WOMEN	
○ SINGLE SCULLS	E.Lipa (ROM)
①	Time:
○ DOUBLE SCULLS	K.Köppen & K.Boron (GER)
①	Time:
○ QUADRUPLE SCULLS	GER
①	Time:
○ COXLESS PAIRS	M.McBean & K.Heddle (CAN)
①	Time:
○ EIGHTS	CAN
①	Time:
○ LIGHTWEIGHT DOUBLE SCULLS	NEW EVENT
①	Time:

EQUESTRIAN EVENTS

THE FIRST equestrian event in the ancient Olympics was a four-horse chariot race, in 680 BC. In the modern Games, a show jumping competition was first held in 1900, and included high jumps and long jumps. The dressage and three-day events were added in 1912. There are individual and team competitions in all three events, and in all three men and women compete together. In the team events, four riders take part, and the scores of the top three count towards the final score.

In the show jumping, competitors tackle a course of 12 to 15 obstacles. They must try to avoid collecting penalty points, called "faults", given for various mistakes, including knocking down fence poles. Speed is also important; if competitors have the same number of faults, the fastest time wins.

In the dressage competition, the riders make their horses perform a variety of paces, halts, direction changes, movements and figures. This disciplined event requires great cooperation between horse and rider. A panel of judges awards points out of 10 for each skill.

The three-day event is made up of three separate competitions — dressage, endurance and show jumping — with points added together. Each competitor must ride the same horse for all the competitions. The endurance competition has four phases. The first and third phases, called "roads and tracks", consist of a trot and a slow canter over a marked course. The second phase is a steeplechase over seven or eight fences around a grass track. The fourth phase is a cross-country ride, with over 30 jumps. In Atlanta, the horses will cover over 21 kilometres, and extra breaks have been introduced to help prevent them overheating in the hot, humid climate.

TEAM	1992 WINNERS
○ SHOW JUMPING	NED

1   Points:
2   Points:
3   Points:

○ DRESSAGE	GER

1   Points:
2   Points:
3   Points:

○ 3-DAY EVENT	AUS

1   Points:
2   Points:
3   Points:

SHOW-JUMPING FAULTS

If a horse knocks down part of an obstacle (1), the competitor collects four faults. A refusal (2) collects three faults, a second refusal collects six faults and a third gets disqualification. If a horse puts a foot in the water or on the tape that marks the edge of the water jump (3), four faults are awarded.

COOLING DOWN

The water is one of the most popular parts of the cross-country course — for spectators anyway! Here Blyth Tait of New Zealand and Messiah negotiate the water at Barcelona (*right*). Tait won individual bronze and team silver in 1992.

CLEAR ROUND

Jos Lansink of the Netherlands (*left*) was in the winning show-jumping team in Barcelona. He also won the 1994 show-jumping World Cup Final, which was held in his own country, collecting no faults at all.

DID YOU KNOW?

● The term "dressage" comes from the French word for "preparation".

● Britain's Lorna Johnstone became the oldest female Olympian ever when she came twelfth in the 1972 dressage; she was 70 years old.

● In 1936, Otomar Bures of Czechoslovakia took over two hours to catch his horse after a fall in the cross-country; he ended up with over 18,000 penalty points!

INDIVIDUAL	1992 WINNERS
○ SHOW JUMPING	L.Beerbaum (GER)
① Points:	
② Points:	
③ Points:	
○ DRESSAGE	N.Uphoff (GER)
① Points:	
② Points:	
③ Points:	
○ 3-DAY EVENT	M.Ryan (AUS)
① Points:	
② Points:	
③ Points:	

GOLD-MEDAL PARTNERSHIP

Nicole Uphoff of Germany and her horse Rembrandt (*right*) have collected four Olympic gold medals in the dressage events. Performing in perfect partnership, they won the individual and the team events at both Seoul and Barcelona. Overall, Germany leads the world in equestrian Olympic gold medals, with a total of 27. Sweden are second, with 17 golds, and France third, with 11.

CYCLING HAS featured in every modern Olympic Games, but Atlanta's programme is very different from that of Athens a hundred years ago. Then six races were ridden by just 19 cyclists from five countries. The first road race, from Athens to Marathon and back, was won by local hero Aristidis Konstantinidis, who won gold on a cycle borrowed from a spectator as he had wrecked his own machine! Women's cycling was introduced to the Games in 1984. Today there are three types of cycling event: track, road racing and mountain biking.

Five men's races and three women's races take place on a track in the cycling stadium, or velodrome. The track is 333 metres round and has high banks on the curves. The individual sprint covers three laps of the track and is a tactical race, with riders trying to outwit each other and then sprinting the last 200 metres. The men's one-kilometre time trial is a track race against the clock. In the individual and team pursuits, two cyclists or two teams of four start at opposite sides of the velodrome — half the track distance apart — and chase (or pursue) each other. The aim is to catch up with the opposition or, if not, to complete the distance in a faster time. In the men's 50-kilometre points race, points are awarded to the leaders after every five laps. The cyclist with most points overall wins.

The road-racing events comprise individual races and time trials for men and women. In the past, time trials on the road have been for teams, but in Atlanta they are individual.

Also new for Atlanta are the cross-country mountain-bike races. This is one of the fastest-growing sports, and the Olympic events will create great interest all round the world. A special wooded, hilly, 12-kilometre course has been made, with races for 50 men and 30 women. This is certain to be one of the most exciting innovations at the 1996 Games.

LONE BREAK

Kathryn Watt of Australia won the women's road race in 1992 by making a break from the pack on the last lap of the 16-km circuit (*left*). This took the other riders by surprise, and the Australian beat the vastly experienced Jeannie Longo of France by 20 seconds.

MEN	1992 WINNERS
○ SPRINT: 3 laps	J.Fiedler (GER)
①	Time:
○ TIME TRIAL: 1 km	J.Moreno Perinan (ESP)
①	Time:
○ INDIV. PURSUIT: 4000 m	C.Boardman (GBR)
①	Time:
○ TEAM PURSUIT: 4000 m	GER
①	Time:
○ POINTS RACE: 50 km	G.Lombardi (ITA)
①	Points:
○ ROAD RACE: 195 km	F.Casartelli (ITA)
①	Time:
○ ROAD TIME TRIAL	NEW EVENT
①	Time:
○ MOUNTAIN BIKE CROSS-COUNTRY	NEW EVENT
①	Time:
WOMEN	**1992 WINNERS**
○ SPRINT: 3 laps	E.Salumae (EST)
①	Time:
○ INDIVIDUAL PURSUIT: 3000 m	P.Rossner (GER)
①	Time:
○ POINTS RACE: 24 km	NEW EVENT
①	Points:
○ ROAD RACE: 70 km	K.Watt (AUS)
①	Time:
○ ROAD TIME TRIAL	NEW EVENT
①	Time:
○ MOUNTAIN BIKE CROSS-COUNTRY	NEW EVENT
①	Time:

TRIALLING TIME

José Manuel Moreno Perinan of Spain won the 1.0 km time trial in the Barcelona velodrome in a time of 63.342 seconds (*right*). Track races can be so close that they are timed to the thousandth of a second.

"DREAM MACHINE"

Britain's Chris Boardman won individual pursuit gold in Barcelona on a revolutionary bike (*below*). He caught the world champion Jens Lehmann of Germany with just under 250 m to go. His carbon fibre cycle, with parts made of titanium and aluminium, weighed just 8.0 kg. It had a raised seat and unusual handlebars, and with Boardman on board it went like a dream!

QUIZ . . . .

1 Which country has won most Olympic cycling medals?
  a) Italy
  b) France
  c) Great Britain

2 When was the last Olympic tandem race held?
  a) 1972
  b) 1906
  c) it never was held!

Answers on page 80

TOUGH MOUNTAIN BIKING

Can Henrik Djernis of Denmark, winner of the 1994 world championships in Vail, Colorado (*below*, centre), win the first cross-country gold?

SHOOTING

SHOOTING HAS been an Olympic sport since 1896. Women first competed alongside men in 1968, and in 1984 separate events for women were also introduced. In 1996, there are no mixed shooting events.

In most events the competitors shoot at a fixed target from a set distance. In the rapid fire pistol event they have to shoot 30 shots first in eight seconds, then six, then four. In the trap and skeet events they fire a shotgun at moving, saucer-shaped clay targets whose flight is similar to a bird taking off, hence the term "clay pigeon shooting", which is sometimes used to describe the sport. In the trap event, 125 clay birds are released from ground level, one at a time and at different angles. In the skeet event 125 clays are released one or two at a time from raised towers and the competitors shoot from eight different stations.

EYES ON THE TARGET

Iouri Fedkine of the Unified Team (*right*) wears the equipment commonly used by crack shots. Eye blinkers shield his eyes from changes in the light. The black square obscures vision from one eye, and the glass lens over the other eye brings into focus the front and rear sights and the bullseye at the same time.

WOMEN	1992 WINNERS
○ PISTOL MATCH: 60 shots at 25 m	M.Logvinenko (EUN)
1	Points:
○ AIR RIFLE: 40 shots at 10 m	Y.Kab-soon (KOR)
1	Points:
○ AIR PISTOL: 40 shots at 10 m	M.Logvinenko (EUN)
1	Points:
○ SMALL BORE RIFLE 3 positions: 20 shots each position at 50 m	L.Melli (USA)
1	Points:
○ DOUBLE TRAP: 120 clays; 1 shot at each	NEW EVENT
1	Points:

FIRING POSITIONS

In the men's three-position small bore rifle event, competitors shoot at a target 50 m away. They fire 40 shots each from three positions: standing (1), kneeling (2) and prone (3).

MEN	1992 WINNERS
○ FREE PISTOL: 60 shots at 50 m	K.Loukachik (EUN)
1	Points:
○ RAPID FIRE PISTOL: 60 shots at 25m	R.Schumann (GER)
1	Points:
○ SMALL BORE RIFLE, prone: 60 shots at 50 m	L.Eun-Chul (KOR)
1	Points:
○ SMALL BORE RIFLE, 3 positions: 40 shots each position at 50 m	G.Petikiane (EUN)
1	Points:
○ RUNNING GAME TARGET: 30 shots at 10 m	M.Jakosits (GER)
1	Points:
○ AIR RIFLE: 60 shots at 10 m	I.Fedkine (EUN)
1	Points:
○ AIR PISTOL: 60 shots at 10 m	W.Yifu (CHN)
1	Points:
○ TRAP: 125 clays; 2 shots at each	NEW EVENT
1	Points:
○ DOUBLE TRAP: 150 clays; 1 shot at each	NEW EVENT
1	Points:
○ SKEET: 125 clays; shot at from 8 stations	NEW EVENT
1	Points:

ARCHERY

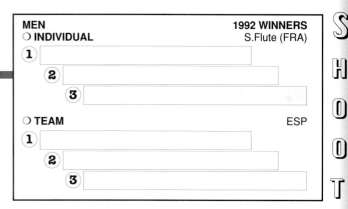

MEN	1992 WINNERS
○ INDIVIDUAL	S.Flute (FRA)
1	
2	
3	
○ TEAM	ESP
1	
2	
3	

WOMEN	1992 WINNERS
○ INDIVIDUAL	C.Youn-Jeong (KOR)
1	
2	
3	
○ TEAM	KOR
1	
2	
3	

ARCHERY MUST be one of the oldest sports in the world, and it became an Olympic sport in 1900. Surprisingly, it was left out of the Games from 1924 to 1968 due to lack of interest. Separate team competitions were introduced in 1988.

HIGH-TECH BOW

Bows used in the Olympics are sophisticated pieces of equipment (*below left*). They are usually made of layers of wood, carbon fibre and ceramic, built up to give as much strength and flexibility as possible. Stabilizers on the front of the bow help to balance it as the archer takes aim, as shown in the picture of Sebastien Flute of France (*below*). They also stop it from twisting when the arrow is released. Arrows are made of aluminium, carbon fibre or a mixture of both. They can fly towards the target at speeds of over 240 kph!

BULLSEYE!

For men, the target (*left*) is placed at 90 m, 70 m, 50 m and 30 m; for women at 70 m, 60 m, 50 m and 30 m. It consists of 10 rings, including the bullseye. An arrow in the bullseye scores 10 points, in the outer gold nine, inner red eight, outer red seven, and so on down to one point for an outer white. In the first round, each archer shoots 36 arrows at each distance. Elimination rounds then determine the eight archers who go through to the finals.

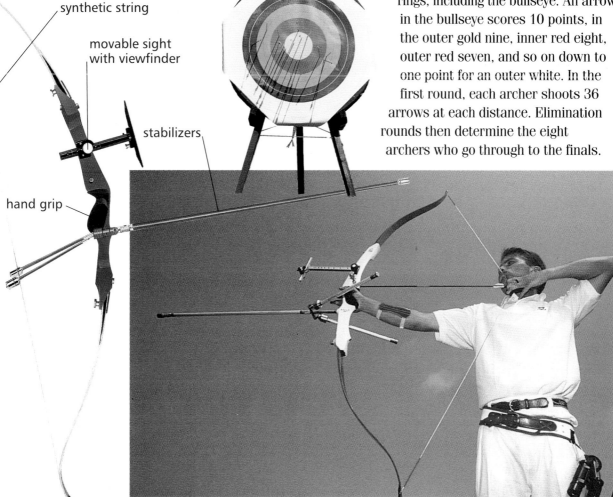

synthetic string

movable sight with viewfinder

stabilizers

hand grip

FENCING

THE SPORT of fencing grew out of the practice of duelling. In a duel, sword fighters would defend their honour by trying to kill or injure their opponent. The idea of modern fencing is not, of course, to injure the opponent, but to hit the other person and avoid being hit oneself. The weapons used have blunt tips and are much lighter than real fighting swords. Safety is all-important: fencers wear a mask, padded jacket, trousers and a glove on the fighting hand.

Fencing has been included in all modern Olympic Games since 1896. Women first competed in 1924. To score points, the fencer must hit certain target areas on the opponent's body. Electronic scoring was introduced in 1936; wires attached to the fencers electronically record hits to the target area. The competitions include both individual and team events for men and women. Men fence with three weapons: the foil, épée and sabre. In the past women used only the foil, but in Atlanta they will fence with the épée too.

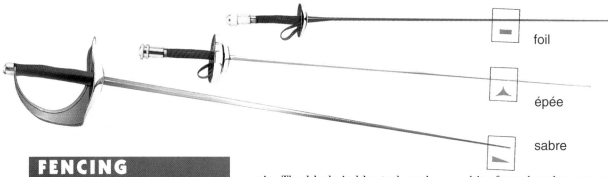

foil

épée

sabre

FENCING WEAPONS

The foil (*top*) is used by men and women. It may be up to 110 cm in length and weigh up to 500 g, but fencers often prefer to use a lighter version. It has a four-sided blade that is rectangular in cross section, a circular hand guard and a handle with a grip. The blade is blunted, and the valid target area is the top half of the opponent's body.

The épée (*centre*) is the same length as the foil, but can weigh up to 770 g. Its blade is triangular in cross section, making it stiffer, and it has a larger hand guard. The target area is the whole body, with hits from head to toe counting as touches.

The sabre (*bottom*) is up to 105 cm long and weighs up to 500 g. Its blade is V-shaped and narrow, and it is the only weapon that scores points by cutting or slicing, as well as thrusting. The target is the entire body above the waist, including the arms.

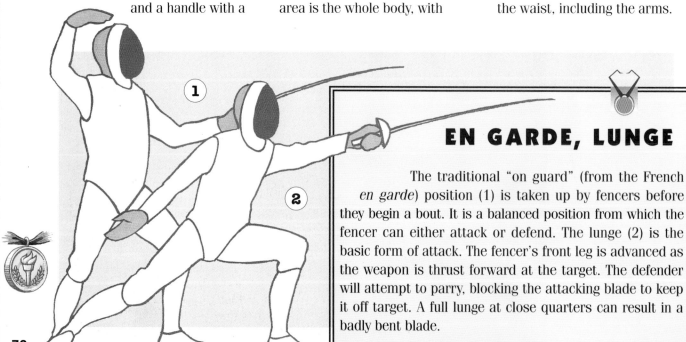

1

2

EN GARDE, LUNGE

The traditional "on guard" (from the French *en garde*) position (1) is taken up by fencers before they begin a bout. It is a balanced position from which the fencer can either attack or defend. The lunge (2) is the basic form of attack. The fencer's front leg is advanced as the weapon is thrust forward at the target. The defender will attempt to parry, blocking the attacking blade to keep it off target. A full lunge at close quarters can result in a badly bent blade.

WOMAN FENCER OF '92

Giovanna Trillini of Italy (*below, right*) won the women's individual foil event in Barcelona. She was also one of the five Italian women who won the team gold medal, beating Germany into second place.

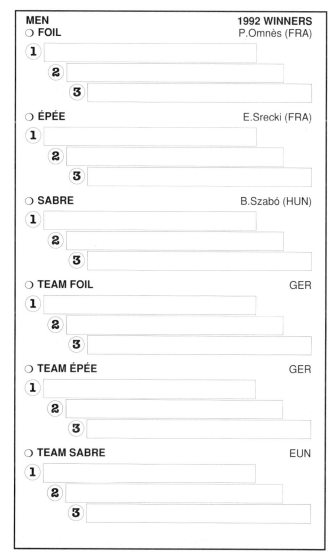

LONG-STANDING RIVALS

Eric Srecki of France (*above*) won gold in the men's individual épée in 1992. France, Hungary and Italy are fierce rivals; they are the top three nations in the medals table. The wire attached to each fencer's body electronically records a hit from his opponent.

MEN	1992 WINNERS
○ FOIL	P.Omnès (FRA)
①	
②	
③	
○ ÉPÉE	E.Srecki (FRA)
①	
②	
③	
○ SABRE	B.Szabó (HUN)
①	
②	
③	
○ TEAM FOIL	GER
①	
②	
③	
○ TEAM ÉPÉE	GER
①	
②	
③	
○ TEAM SABRE	EUN
①	
②	
③	

WOMEN	1992 WINNERS
○ FOIL	G.Trillini (ITA)
①	
②	
③	
○ TEAM FOIL	ITA
①	
②	
③	
○ ÉPÉE	NEW EVENT
①	
②	
③	
○ TEAM ÉPÉE	NEW EVENT
①	
②	
③	

DID YOU KNOW ?

● Fencing is one of only five sports to have been part of every modern Olympics.

● Aladár Gerevich of Hungary, who at 50 was the oldest fencing gold medallist, won seven golds, a silver and two bronzes in his career.

MODERN PENTATHLON

THE FIRST pentathlon, which means "five contests", was contested at the eighteenth ancient Olympics in 708 BC. The new event was included at the insistence of warriors from Sparta in Greece. They were looking for a tough competition for their young men, who received strict military training from the age of seven. The pentathlon was designed to test the all-round ability of the soldier athlete and was an elimination contest. All athletes took part in the first event, the long jump. Those who gained a certain distance went on to the spear-throwing contest. The four best throwers qualified for the sprint race. The fastest three sprinters then threw the discus, and the top two discus throwers finally wrestled each other to decide the overall pentathlon champion.

The modern pentathlon ("modern" as opposed to "ancient") is rather different! It was introduced in 1912, and was loosely based on the tests that a military messenger of past times might have faced. The idea was that the messenger rode over obstacles on a strange horse, was challenged by an enemy soldier with a sword, swam across a river, fought his way with a pistol and finally ran to deliver his message. This imaginary adventure is the basis for the five parts of the modern pentathlon, a men-only event. The five parts are: equestrian, fencing, swimming, shooting and running.

Since 1956 the scoring system has been similar to the track and field decathlon and heptathlon. Competitors are awarded points for their performance in each discipline. An additional team competition was introduced in 1952, but this has not been included in the Atlanta Olympic Games.

○ **MODERN PENTATHLON '92 WINNER** A.Skrzypaszek (POL) **OLYMPIC RECORD** A.Starostin (URS) 5568	
①	Points:
②	Points:
③	Points:

THE FIVE CONTESTS

For the equestrian event, horses that are considered of equal ability are selected beforehand, and are drawn at random by the competitors. Each rider is given 20 minutes to practise riding his horse. The show-jumping course is 600 m long, with 15 obstacles to jump. Points are given according to the number of faults gained and time taken to complete the round. Here Edouard Zenovka of the Unified Team (*left*) takes his horse through its paces at Barcelona.

In the fencing competition, each competitor fences all the others in a duel with épées (see page 76). Electrical touch-recorders are used to detect when each fencer touches the other with his sword, and a competitor wins a duel when he scores a touch. If no touch is made after two minutes, the duel counts as a loss for both fencers. Points are scored according to the number of duels won.

Competitors in the swimming event each swim 300 m freestyle. Points are awarded according to the time taken. Zenovka (*right*) is again seen in action.

CHAMPION PENTATHLETE

Arkadiusz Skrzypaszek of Poland (*left*) scored a total of 5559 points, to win the modern pentathlon at the Barcelona Olympics. He was very consistent in all five disciplines and won the gold medal without coming first in any of the individual events. Followers of the modern pentathlon consider it to be the supreme test of all-round athletes (though the decathletes might disagree!).

QUIZ . . . .

1 How many lengths of the Olympic pool is the pentathlon swimming race?
    a) 4
    b) 5
    c) 6

2 Which country do you think has won most modern pentathlon medals?
    a) Sweden
    b) Greece
    c) Poland

3 How many events are there in total in the pentathlon, heptathlon and decathlon?
    a) 20
    b) 22
    c) 24

Answers on page 80

In the shooting competition, competitors fire .22-calibre pistols at targets from a distance of 25 m. The targets are 50-cm circles, and each competitor has four rounds of five shots each. Pentathlon points are given according to the target points scored.

The cross-country run takes place over a 4000-m course. Competitors are allowed to look at the course before the race, and they start at 30-second intervals. Points are awarded according to each runner's time. A time of 14 minutes 15 seconds wins 1000 points; every second faster or slower than this time gains or loses three points. Here, Zenovka (*right*) heads for the finish in the last part of the modern pentathlon at Barcelona.

MODERN PENTATHLON

ANSWERS

page 7:	1 b; 2 a; 3 c.	
page 11:	1 a; 2 c; 3 b.	
page 21:	1 b; 2 c; 3 a.	
page 25:	1 c; 2 b; 3 a.	
page 33:	1 b; 2 a; 3 c.	
page 45:	1 c; 2 b; 3 a.	
page 51:	1 b; 2 c; 3 a.	
page 55:	1 a; 2 c; 3 b.	
page 61:	1 a; 2 b; 3 c.	
page 73:	1 b; 2 a.	
page 79:	1 c; 2 a; 3 b.	
Total points		

Score one point for each correct answer.

How did you do?

30-32 points: gold-medal winning performance!

26-29 points: silver medal

22-25 points: bronze medal

18-21 points: just outside the medals

10-17 points: at the back of the field

0-9 points: you never got out of the starting blocks!

Units of measurement	
1 cm	= 0.39 in
1 m	= 3.28 ft
1 km	= 0.62 mi
1 sq m	= 10.76 sq ft
1 g	= 0.04 oz
1 kg	= 2.21 lbs

Some former Olympic teams	
EUN	Unified Team
FRG	West Germany
GDR	East Germany
TCH	Czechoslovakia
URS	Soviet Union

ABBREVIATIONS FOR COUNTRIES IN THE OLYMPIC GAMES

AFG	Afghanistan	CYP	Cyprus	KSA	Saudi Arabia	ROM	Romania
AHO	Netherlands Antilles	CZE	Czech Republic	KUW	Kuwait	RSA	South Africa
ALB	Albania	DEN	Denmark	LAO	Laos	RUS	Russia
ALG	Algeria	DJI	Djibouti	LAT	Latvia	RWA	Rwanda
AND	Andorra	DMA	Dominica	LBA	Libya	SAM	Western Samoa
ANG	Angola	DOM	Dominican Republic	LBR	Liberia	SEN	Senegal
ANT	Antigua	ECU	Ecuador	LCA	St Lucia	SEY	Seychelles
ARG	Argentina	EGY	Egypt	LES	Lesotho	SIN	Singapore
ARM	Armenia	ESA	El Salvador	LIB	Lebanon	SKN	St Kitts & Nevis
ARU	Aruba	ESP	Spain	LIE	Liechtenstein	SLE	Sierra Leone
ASA	American Samoa	EST	Estonia	LTU	Lithuania	SLO	Slovenia
AUS	Australia	ETH	Ethiopia	LUX	Luxembourg	SMR	San Marino
AUT	Austria	FIJ	Fiji	MAD	Madagascar	SOL	Solomon Islands
AZE	Azerbaijan	FIN	Finland	MAR	Morocco	SOM	Somalia
BAH	Bahamas	FRA	France	MAS	Malaysia	SRI	Sri Lanka
BAN	Bangladesh	GAB	Gabon	MAW	Malawi	STP	São Tomé & Principe
BAR	Barbados	GAM	Gambia	MDA	Moldova	SUD	Sudan
BDI	Burundi	GBR	Great Britain	MDV	Maldives	SUI	Switzerland
BEL	Belgium	GBS	Guinea-Bissau	MEX	Mexico	SUR	Suriname
BEN	Benin	GEO	Georgia	MGL	Mongolia	SVK	Slovakia
BER	Bermuda	GEQ	Equatorial Guinea	MKD	Macedonia	SWE	Sweden
BHU	Bhutan	GER	Germany	MLI	Mali	SWZ	Swaziland
BIH	Bosnia & Herzegovina	GHA	Ghana	MLT	Malta	SYR	Syria
BIZ	Belize	GRE	Greece	MON	Monaco	TAN	Tanzania
BLR	Belarus	GRN	Grenada	MOZ	Mozambique	TGA	Tonga
BOL	Bolivia	GUA	Guatemala	MRI	Mauritius	THA	Thailand
BOT	Botswana	GUI	Guinea	MTN	Mauritania	TJK	Tajikistan
BRA	Brazil	GUM	Guam	MYA	Myanmar	TKM	Turkmenistan
BRN	Bahrain	GUY	Guyana	NAM	Namibia	TOG	Togo
BRU	Brunei	HAI	Haiti	NCA	Nicaragua	TPE	Taiwan
BUL	Bulgaria	HKG	Hong Kong	NED	Netherlands	TRI	Trinidad & Tobago
BUR	Burkina Faso	HON	Honduras	NEP	Nepal	TUN	Tunisia
CAF	Central African Republic	HUN	Hungary	NGR	Nigeria	TUR	Turkey
		INA	Indonesia	NIG	Niger	UAE	United Arab Emirates
CAM	Cambodia	IND	India	NOR	Norway	UGA	Uganda
CAN	Canada	IRI	Iran	NRU	Nauru	UKR	Ukraine
CAY	Cayman Islands	IRL	Ireland	NZL	New Zealand	URU	Uruguay
CGO	Congo	IRQ	Iraq	OMA	Oman	USA	United States of America
CHA	Chad	ISL	Iceland	PAK	Pakistan		
CHI	Chile	ISR	Israel	PAN	Panama	UZB	Uzbekistan
CHN	China	ISV	Virgin Islands	PAR	Paraguay	VAN	Vanuatu
CIV	Ivory Coast	ITA	Italy	PER	Peru	VEN	Venezuela
CMR	Cameroon	IVB	British Virgin Islands	PHI	Philippines	VIE	Vietnam
COK	Cook Islands	JAM	Jamaica	PLE	Palestine (provisional)	VIN	St Vincent & Grenadines
COL	Colombia	JOR	Jordan	PNG	Papua New Guinea		
COM	Comoros	JPN	Japan	POL	Poland	YEM	Yemen
CPV	Cape Verde	KAZ	Kazakhstan	POR	Portugal	YUG	Yugoslavia
CRC	Costa Rica	KEN	Kenya	PRK	North Korea	ZAI	Zaire
CRO	Croatia	KGZ	Kyrgyzstan	PUR	Puerto Rico	ZAM	Zambia
CUB	Cuba	KOR	South Korea	QAT	Qatar	ZIM	Zimbabwe